ALSO BY DR. KATE BIBERDORF

Kate the Chemist: The Big Book of Experiments

THE KATE THE CHEMIST NOVELS:

Kate the Chemist: Dragons vs. Unicorns

Kate the Chemist: The Great Escape

Kate the Chemist: The STEM Night Disaster

Kate the Chemist: The Birthday Blastoff

The AWESOME BOOK of EDIBLE EXPERIMENTS for KIDS

DR. KATE BIBERDORF

PHILOMEL BOOKS

PHILOMEL BOOKS
An imprint of Penguin Random House LLC, New York

First published in the United States of America by Philomel Books,
an imprint of Penguin Random House LLC, 2021.

Philomel Books is a registered trademark of Penguin Random House LLC.

Visit us online at penguinrandomhouse.com

Library of Congress Cataloging-in-Publication Data is available.

Manufactured in China

ISBN 9780593116197

10 9 8 7 6 5 4 3 2 1

Edited by Jill Santopolo.
Design by Lori Thorn.
Text set in ITC Stone Serif.

For my sous-chef, Josh.

SAFETY ICONS

HEAT GLOVES/OVEN MITTS

LATEX GLOVES

ADULT NEEDED

CONTENTS

INTRODUCTION

Hi! My name is Dr. Kate Biberdorf, but most people call me Kate the Chemist. You can usually find me teaching classes in Austin, Texas, or setting off explosions on national TV. Last year, I published my first nonfiction book (*The Big Book of Experiments*), which contained 25 at-home experiments, including one of my favorites, Edible Snot. People loved that demo so much that my inbox exploded with requests for more experiments that can be done in the kitchen—so I set off on a flour-filled adventure to create 25 new EDIBLE science experiments.

From Unicorn Sugar Cookies to Dragon Cupcakes, every protocol is packed full of chemistry. Do you know what chemistry is, besides being the best science in the entire world? It's the study of energy and matter, and their interactions with each other. Like how the proteins in our flour react with the sugars in our dough to give us a brown pretzel, or how salt can lower the temperature of a milk mixture to give us ice cream (two things I show you how to do in this book)!

Each experiment can be done with materials that your parents or guardians probably already have in their pantry (like sugar, baking soda, and food coloring). But the best part is, unlike my last book, you can actually eat every single one of these final products! Chemistry is everywhere in the kitchen, which is why I had so much fun creating all of these recipes for you. So what are you waiting for? Call your bestie, grab your apron—it's time for kitchen chemistry!

XOXO,
Kate

FRY AN EGG

A NOTE FROM KATE: Fried eggs have always intimidated me. They cook very quickly and if you get distracted for even a minute, you can ruin your egg. The good news is that eggs usually come in a 12-pack, so you can just crack another egg and do your experiment over again (and again and again . . .) if you need to.

MESSINESS LEVEL: 2/3

MATERIALS:

- ○ Large nonstick skillet (or cast-iron pan) with lid
- ○ Stove
- ○ 2 tablespoons butter
- ○ Spatula
- ○ 2 eggs
- ○ Small bowl

EXPERIMENT A—SLOW-COOKED EGG

PROtOCOL:

1. Heat the pan over medium heat for 3–5 minutes. Make sure the pan is hot before moving to the next step.
2. Add the butter to the pan. Use the spatula to coat the bottom of the pan with the butter.
3. Break 1 egg into the small bowl and remove any eggshells.
4. Use the small bowl to gently add the egg to the pan.
5. Cook for about 90 seconds (until the egg white is opaque). Cover the pan with the lid.
6. Reduce the heat to low and cook for 4 more minutes.
7. Remove the pan from the heat and enjoy your egg!

EXPERIMENT B—FAST-COOKED EGG

PROtOCOL:

1. Heat the pan over medium heat for 3–5 minutes. Make sure the pan is hot before moving to the next step.
2. Add the butter to the pan. Use the spatula to coat the bottom of the pan with the butter.
3. Break the egg into the small bowl and remove any eggshells.
4. Use the small bowl to gently add the egg to the pan. Cover the pan with the lid.
5. Cook for about 2 minutes (until the egg white is opaque).
6. Remove the pan from the heat and let the egg sit for 30 seconds (still covered).
7. Remove the lid and enjoy your egg!

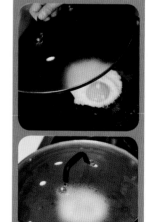

WHAT DO YOU THINK?

> Why is it important to heat the pan before we add the butter?
> Why do we cover the pan with the lid?
> Would it be possible to cook 2 or 3 eggs at the same time? Why or why not?
> Which method gave us a better fried egg? Why do you think that is?

HOW It WORKS:

In this quick and easy experiment, we start off by heating the pan for a few minutes. Even though it's hard to wait, this step is crucial because we need the egg to receive the exact same amount of heat from every inch of the pan. This ensures that we uniformly cook the molecules inside the egg, which are separated into two sacks of proteins: the egg white and egg yolk.

When these proteins interact with heat, they change the orientation of the molecule. This process is called denaturation, where the proteins go from a folded position to an unfolded position. When I think of this process, I imagine the proteins moving from the tuck position to a snow angel position whenever they go through this reaction. As soon as the protein has opened up, the liquid (inedible) egg can then be converted into the solid (tasty) egg. This happens during both experiments when the egg turns from translucent to white or from dark yellow to that classic egg-yolk yellow. Experiment B rushes this process along, which is why it typically does not generate a fried egg as tasty as the one produced from Experiment A.

You may have noticed that the egg whites started to turn into a solid at around 63°C (145°F), whereas the egg yolks needed to be heated to about 70°C (158°F). If we had whisked these two sets of proteins together (like when making scrambled eggs or omelets), new bonds would have formed between the egg whites and egg yolks that make the egg more stable (chemically). I can prove this to you because you should be able to heat an egg white/ yolk mixture to almost 73°C (163°F). Luckily for us, egg bacteria cannot live at these temperatures, which means it is safe for us to eat the fried eggs!

HOT SAUCE

A NOTE FROM Kate: My husband and I love spicy food, which means we always have hot peppers in our house and our food is never bland. Fair warning, this experiment is going to test your limits! If you do not like spicy food, you may want to skip this one.

MESSINESS LEVEL: 2/3

MATERIALS:

- ○ 1 green bell pepper
- ○ 1 red bell pepper
- ○ 1 poblano pepper
- ○ 1 jalapeño pepper
- ○ Knife
- ○ Cutting board
- ○ 1 glass whole milk
- ○ 5 peppers (of your desired heat)
- ○ Medium (or large) saucepan + lid
- ○ ¾ cup apple cider vinegar
- ○ ½ teaspoon salt
- ○ 2 teaspoons minced garlic
- ○ Stove
- ○ Immersion blender (or regular blender)
- ○ Goggles (optional)

PROTOCOL:

1. Make a label for each pepper.

2. *Ask an adult to help you with this step.* Wearing gloves, cut a 1 cm x 1 cm piece of each pepper and put it on its label. Be sure to remove any seeds from the pepper.
   PRO TIP: Do not touch your eyes after touching hot peppers. It will sting!

PROTOCOL (CONTINUED):

3. Eat the red bell pepper **slowly**. Make sure your glass of milk is nearby.

4. Analyze the texture and heat of the pepper.

5. Repeat steps 3–4 for the remaining peppers in this order: green bell, poblano, jalapeño. If your mouth feels like it's on fire, you can take a sip of milk to help with the heat.

6. Use the results to determine which pepper you like the best, and use it for the remainder of this experiment.

7. *Ask an adult to help you with this step.* Wearing gloves, cut the tops off 5 of your favorite peppers (mine are jalapeño).

8. Cut the peppers in half (keep the seeds with the peppers this time) and put them into the saucepan.
CAUTION: Be careful if you use a lot of hot peppers. The capsaicin can make you cough if you breathe it in directly.

9. Add the vinegar, salt, and garlic to the saucepan and stir.

10. Bring the mixture to a boil before reducing the heat to low.

11. Cover and heat for 10 minutes (or until the peppers are tender).

12. Use an immersion blender (or pour the mixture into a regular blender).
PRO TIP: I like to wear my lab goggles for this step to make sure I don't get any hot sauce in my eyes.

13. Blend until a homogenous mixture has formed, where everything looks the same.

14. Taste your hot sauce and see what you think. If you want more heat, add another pepper! If it needs more salt, add some salt. If you want a little more tang, add a little vinegar. You can make the hot sauce taste exactly the way you like it best. Enjoy the best part of being a scientist.

WHAT DO YOU THINK?

> Why did we start our taste test with the bell pepper instead of the jalapeño pepper?
> Why did we wear gloves when working with the peppers?
> Why did we use apple cider vinegar instead of white vinegar in the hot sauce?
> What will happen if we add a Thai pepper or habanero (or a ghost pepper!) to the hot sauce?

HOW IT WORKS:

When I moved across the country (from Michigan to Texas), I had no idea how little I knew about peppers. But after living in the South for twelve years, I have slowly been introduced to an entirely new world of hot peppers. Each pepper can be ranked by its spiciness with something called the Scoville scale (a scale created by a pharmacist named Wilbur Scoville). With this scale, we can arrange all known peppers by the amount of heat components in each pepper.

But how do we actually do that? In Scoville's organoleptic test (using our sense organs), we dissolve the hot pepper in an alcohol to remove the capsaicinoids (a group of molecules that provide heat to peppers). This spicy alcohol mixture is then diluted into a sugar-water solution and tested for its heat components. Water is continuously added to the mixture, until the spiciness from the peppers can no longer be detected. The heat from the hottest chili peppers (like ghost peppers) can be detected after *a lot* of water has been added.

The main molecule that we detect in spicy foods is called capsaicin. It's a long molecule that is mostly found in chili peppers, but you may also see it in topical creams that help to alleviate arthritic joint pain. Capsaicin is nonpolar, therefore it readily dissolves in other nonpolar liquids. When we drink milk after eating hot peppers, we are actually dissolving the capsaicin molecules into the nonpolar fats found in milk. That's why we used the fattiest milk (whole milk) in this experiment.

HOLLANDAISE SAUCE

A Note From Kate: Although this sauce sounds French, it is actually a sauce made by my people, the Dutch. The French phrase "sauce Hollandaise" translates to "Dutch sauce," and it is absolutely delicious. The best part about this sauce is that it is so good you can use it at breakfast, lunch, and dinner!

Messiness Level: 2/3

Materials:

- ○ 4 small heat-safe bowls
- ○ 5 eggs
- ○ 4½ teaspoons lemon juice
- ○ Whisk
- ○ 1 cup butter, melted
- ○ Microwave

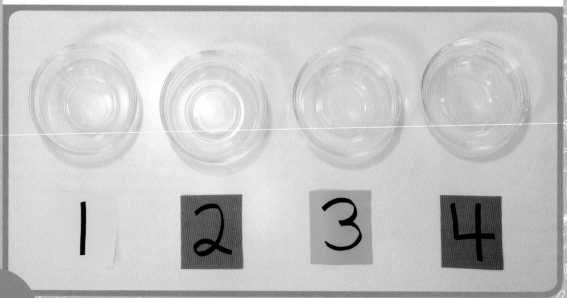

PROTOCOL:

1. Place the four small bowls on the table and label them 1, 2, 3, and 4.

2. Crack one egg and place it in Bowl 1.

3. Crack the second and third eggs. Place the egg whites in Bowl 2 and the egg yolks in Bowl 3.

SEPARATING THE EGG YOLKS FROM THE EGG WHITES

a. Cleanly crack the egg.

b. Holding the egg over the small bowl, open the egg into two halves (allowing any egg white to gently drop into the small bowl).

c. Slowly transfer the egg yolk back and forth between the eggshells, allowing any egg white to gently drop into the bowl.

d. Repeat step 3 until all the egg white is in the bowl and out of the shell.

4. Crack the fourth and fifth eggs, and place the egg yolks in Bowl 4. Discard the egg whites.

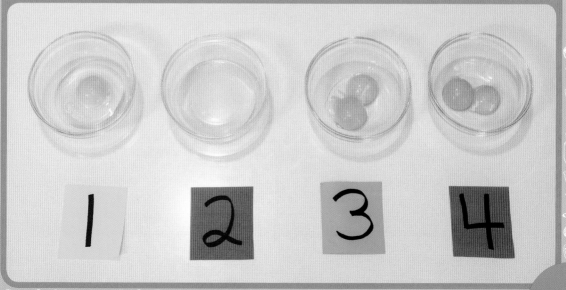

PROTOCOL (CONTINUED):

5. Add 1½ teaspoons of lemon juice to Bowls 1, 2, and 3 (NOT Bowl 4).

6. Whisk together until smooth. (Make sure to wash the whisk between each bowl so you don't contaminate the experiment.)

7. Add ¼ cup of melted butter to Bowls 1, 2, 3, and 4.

8. Whisk together until smooth.

9. Put Bowl 1 in the microwave for 20 seconds.

10. Remove the bowl from the microwave and whisk again to combine. Record the appearance, color, and texture of the mixture. Set aside.

11. Repeat steps 9–10 for Bowl 2.

12. Repeat steps 9–10 for Bowl 3.

13. Repeat steps 9–10 for Bowl 4.

14. Compare the four different sauces.

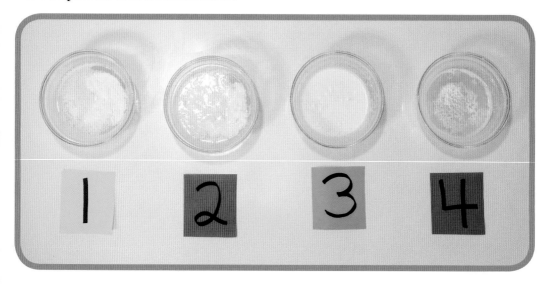

> What is the primary difference between an egg yolk and an egg white?
> Which combination made the best hollandaise sauce? Why do you think that is?
> Does the lemon juice enhance the sauce? Why or why not?
> What will happen if we use orange juice or lime juice instead of lemon juice?

HOW It WORKS:

Eggs whites and egg yolks are both small pouches of proteins that are floating among water molecules. In the egg yolk, there is an extra layer of fat that gives the protein sack its thick, dense physical properties. These fat molecules are nonpolar, so they do not mix well with the polar water molecules. However, when we use a whisk to break up the protein pouches, we can force an emulsion to form. This means that one liquid is suspended within the other liquid. For our experiment, the tiny fat droplets from the egg yolk are dispersed within the water from both protein pouches. However, the distinctive appearance of the hollandaise sauce does not form until the entire mixture has been thoroughly heated.

As we can see from the sauces made in Bowls C and D, the lemon juice is needed in order to make the perfect hollandaise sauce. The citric acid in the lemon wiggles its way into the emulsion to make sure that the proteins in the egg sacks cannot coagulate or solidify (what happens when proteins form strong bonds with one another). Since coagulation mostly happens when the eggs are heated, it's important to vigorously mix the lemon juice into the egg mixture before putting it into the microwave. Otherwise, the fats and water will separate to give us a disgusting, chunky sauce.

If you are up for the challenge, see what other fruits can be used to make the sauce. Try adding orange juice (or grapefruit juice) to see how the texture and flavor change. You can also try most vinegars, but you might have to get creative to mask the strong sour flavors that usually accompany the acetic acid in vinegar.

BUTTERMILK

A Note from Kate: I love the smell, taste, and texture of a good buttermilk biscuit. The problem is, I never seem to have buttermilk in my refrigerator. So, over the years, I have learned how to make buttermilk in a pinch. It's super easy to whip up, which is why you should never let the lack of buttermilk keep you from experimenting in the kitchen!

Messiness Level: 1/3

Materials:

- ◯ 3 cups or glasses
- ◯ 3 cups milk
- ◯ ¼ cup + 1 tablespoon + 1 teaspoon white vinegar

Protocol:

1. Place the three cups on your table and label them A, B, and C.

2. Add 1 cup of milk to each cup.

3. Add 1 teaspoon of white vinegar to Cup A.

4. Add 1 tablespoon of white vinegar to Cup B.

5. Add ¼ cup of white vinegar to Cup C.

6. Wait for 15 minutes.

7. Examine the three different buttermilks.

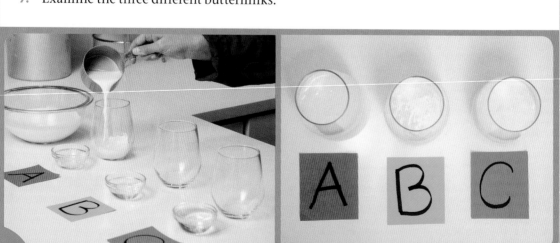

> What happened when the vinegar was initially mixed with the milk?
> What happened to the milk after 15 minutes of chemical reactivity?
> Which of the three ratios is best for the formation of at-home buttermilk?
> When you pour the buttermilk concoctions into an empty cup, what do you see at the bottom of Cups A, B, and C?
> What do you think would happen if you used lemon juice instead of vinegar?

HOW IT WORKS:

The milk we drink is primarily made from water, followed by lactose, fat, and protein. Lactose is a disaccharide (meaning it's made up of two sugars), but it is not nearly as sweet as table sugar. That's one of the reasons why milk doesn't taste anything like lemonade or sweet tea. The fats in the milk are nonpolar, so that means they'll separate from the polar water molecules over time. However, since the concentration of the fat molecules is actually quite small, most people rarely see this happen unless their milk has gone bad.

When the vinegar is added to the milk, the acetic acid molecules drop the pH (a low pH means you have an acidic solution). When these milk proteins are in an acidic environment, they can begin to coagulate (or solidify)—just like what happens when proteins are cooked in the oven. However, instead of browning the exterior of a pie, these proteins begin to curdle (or clump together) inside the milk.

In this experiment, we generated an acidified buttermilk that can be used as a delicious ingredient in biscuits and pancakes. Feel free to experiment in the kitchen to figure out which buttermilk tastes best to you, but I prefer the ratios that we used in Cup B (1 tablespoon of vinegar to 1 cup of milk). At these ratios, the buttermilk is not too sour and it can still act as a leavening agent (like baking powder) to produce carbon dioxide gas when heated in the oven. This chemical reaction is what ultimately gives the buttermilk biscuits the light and fluffy texture that we all know and love.

BANANA BREAD

A NOTE FROM Kate: The best part about banana bread is that you can repurpose any bananas that have over-ripened (turned black) into a deliciously sweet bread. However, whenever I want to make banana bread, I only seem to have fresh, yellow bananas! So, in this experiment, I investigate three different ways of ripening fresh bananas.

MESSINESS LEVEL: 2/3

MATERIALS:

- ○ 7 fresh bananas
- ○ Permanent marker
- ○ Paper bag
- ○ Tape
- ○ Fork
- ○ Microwave
- ○ Oven
- ○ Baking sheet
- ○ Butter for greasing pan (or nonstick cooking spray)
- ○ 9x5-inch bread pan
- ○ Mixing bowl
- ○ ½ cup butter, softened
- ○ ¾ cup brown sugar
- ○ 2 eggs
- ○ ½ cup buttermilk (pick your best cup from the Buttermilk experiment)
- ○ ¾ teaspoon vanilla
- ○ 2 medium bowls
- ○ 2 cups flour
- ○ 1 teaspoon baking soda
- ○ ¼ teaspoon salt
- ○ Cooling rack

PROTOCOL:

1. Label the outsides of 3 fresh bananas with a permanent marker as A, B, and C. Record the appearance and firmness of each banana (and take a picture, if possible).

EXPERIMENT A—BROWN PAPER BAG

PROTOCOL:

1. Place Banana A into a brown bag.

2. Roll the edges of the bag over gently and loosely tape it shut. Set aside for 24 hours.

3. After 24 hours, remove the banana from the bag and compare its appearance to your before photo.

4. Peel the banana and analyze the appearance, firmness, and taste of Banana A.

EXPERIMENT B—MICROWAVE

PROTOCOL:

1. Poke a few holes in Banana B with a fork.

2. Microwave Banana B for 30 seconds.

3. Flip the banana over and microwave for 15 seconds longer.

4. Remove the banana from the microwave and compare its appearance to your before photo.

5. Peel the banana and analyze the appearance, firmness, and taste of Banana B.

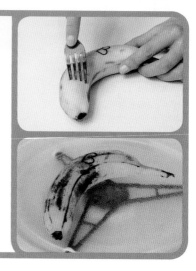

EXPERIMENT C—OVEN

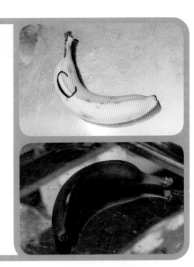

PROTOCOL:

1. Heat the oven to 300°F.

2. Place Banana C on a baking sheet and bake for 20–30 minutes (or until the banana peel is black).

3. Remove the banana from the oven and compare its appearance to your before photo.

4. Peel the banana and analyze the appearance, firmness, and taste of Banana C.

PROTOCOL (CONTINUED):

2. Compare your results to determine which banana had the sweetest taste.

3. Repeat the technique that produced the sweetest banana for 4 fresh bananas. Leave the bananas in the peel (for now). We will use these bananas for the rest of the experiment.

4. Take the butter out of the refrigerator and set aside.

5. Heat the oven to 350°F.

6. Rub the bread pan with butter (or spray with nonstick cooking spray).

7. In the mixing bowl, cream together the butter and brown sugar by hand (or with an electric mixer).

PROTOCOL (CONTINUED):

8. Add the eggs and stir.

9. Add the buttermilk and vanilla and stir.

10. Peel the 4 newly prepared bananas and put them into one of the medium bowls.

11. Use a fork to mash the bananas.

12. Add the bananas to the butter and sugar mixture and stir until you have a homogenous mixture, where everything looks completely mixed together.

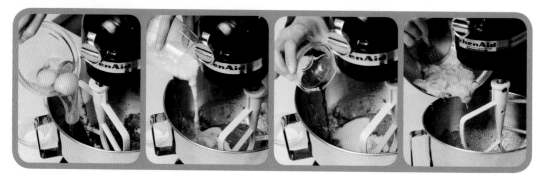

13. In a separate mixing bowl, stir together the flour, baking soda, and salt.

14. Add half of the flour mixture to the banana mixture and stir.

15. Add the remaining flour mixture and stir.

16. Pour the mixture into the prepared bread pan.

17. Bake the bread for 60–75 minutes (or until an inserted toothpick comes out clean).

18. Allow the bread to cool for 15 minutes.

19. Remove the bread from the pan and place it on a cooling rack.

20. Allow it to cool completely before enjoying your bread!

HOW It WORKS:

Bananas are a type of fruit that is categorized as a berry, even though they don't look like what we typically think of as a berry. They tend to grow in groups, and go through classic color changes. When bananas are originally picked, they are deep green in color. Then they are placed in an airtight room before being exposed to ethylene, a molecule that naturally exists in many plants, including bananas. This hormone makes bananas ripen slowly on their trees when bananas are left alone in nature. But when they are completely submerged in ethylene gas, the process happens much faster.

Macroscopically, visible to us without any tools, we can watch this chemical reaction occur when the bananas turn from green to yellow. Microscopically, this means that the ethylene molecules have broken down the bonds within *other* molecules that are within the fruit. For the banana, this means that the big starch molecules have broken down into sweeter sucrose molecules. This is a crucial step in our experiment because it changes the taste of the banana from slightly bitter to sugary and delicious.

When we place Banana A in the paper bag, we trap all of these ethylene gases. This builds up the concentration of the gas and quickens the rate of reaction. Banana A begins to ripen after a few hours, and after 24–48 hours, the entire banana has over-ripened. This exact same process can be expedited with heat (like from a microwave or oven), which is why we were able to achieve the same outcome with Bananas B and C. In nature, this chemical reaction is not meant to occur within a few minutes, so we can usually taste the difference between the sweetness in Banana A and Bananas B and C.

DEFROSTING BERRIES

A NOTE FROM Kate: Growing up in Michigan, I used to pick fresh berries every summer. My mom would freeze a big bag of them so that we could have blueberries in the winter. Nothing was better than warm blueberry muffins in the middle of a blizzard!

MESSINESS LEVEL: 2/3

MATERIALS:
- 3 cups frozen berries
- Heat-safe bowl
- Microwave
- Spoon
- Baking sheet
- Small bowl
- 1 cup ice-cold water
- Dish towel
- Strainer

EXPERIMENT A—MICROWAVE

PROTOCOL:
1. Pour 1 cup of frozen berries into a heat-safe bowl.

2. Put the bowl in the microwave for 30 seconds. Use the defrost setting, if possible.

3. Remove the bowl from the microwave.

4. If the berries are still frozen, gently stir the berries before microwaving them for 10 more seconds.

5. Repeat step 4 until the berries are completely defrosted.

6. Remove the berries from the microwave.

7. Analyze the appearance and texture of the berries.

EXPERIMENT B—ROOM TEMPERATURE

PROTOCOL:

1. Pour 1 cup of frozen berries onto a baking sheet. Make sure the berries are completely separated.

2. Set aside for 10 minutes.

3. Analyze the appearance and texture of the berries.

4. Repeat steps 2 and 3 until one hour has passed (or until berries have completely defrosted).

EXPERIMENT C—COLD WATER BATH

PROTOCOL:

1. Pour 1 cup of frozen berries into a small bowl.

2. Add the cold water to the bowl. Make sure the berries are completely covered with water. If they are not, add more cold water.

3. Cover the bowl with the dish towel. Set aside for 5 minutes.

4. If the berries are still frozen, gently stir the berries before letting them sit for another 5 minutes.

5. Repeat step 4 until the berries are completely defrosted.

6. Using a strainer, filter the berries out of the water.

7. Analyze the appearance and texture of the berries.

HOW IT WORKS:

Fresh and frozen berries are very similar. They contain sugar, vitamins, minerals, and most importantly, water. At the microscopic level, the biggest difference between fresh and frozen berries is the length of the hydrogen bonds that exist between their water molecules. In the liquid phase, these hydrogen bonds are very short, and the water molecules are packed closely together. In the solid phase, these hydrogen bonds are a bit longer, which means that the molecules are spaced farther apart.

What's neat about the small distance between the water molecules in any liquid phase is that it allows for solid ice to float on top of liquid water. Most solids are the exact opposite—they will sink in their liquid—since most solids have shorter distances between their molecules than liquids do. This concept is important in our berry experiment because when water freezes, it expands (most solids shrink).

Fresh berries are approximately 85% water. When they are placed in the freezer, the internal water freezes. The newly formed ice pushes against the edges of the cell membranes, often causing catastrophic damage to the cells. When the berries are removed from the freezer, we can actually observe the effect of the ruptured cell membranes. Since this means that the berry now struggles to retain the water, our previously frozen berries end up looking pretty mangled. However, the one way to prevent complete and total destruction of the cells is by using cold water to defrost the berries. This allows the berries to slowly warm up to room temperature, which ultimately minimizes the amount of damage to the inside of the berry.

BLUEBERRY MUFFINS

A note from Kate: This experiment is so much fun! It can be replicated with any type of berry, but I just love blueberries in my breakfast pastries. If you want to take the recipe up a notch, mix a little bit of sugar, cinnamon, and butter together for a perfect muffin topping!

Messiness Level: 2/3

Materials:

- ○ Oven
- ○ Muffin pan
- ○ Butter for greasing pan (or nonstick cooking spray)
- ○ 2 mixing bowls
- ○ ¼ cup butter, softened
- ○ ¾ cup white sugar
- ○ 1 egg
- ○ ¾ teaspoon vanilla
- ○ Medium bowl
- ○ 1 cup + 2 tablespoons flour
- ○ 1 teaspoon baking powder
- ○ ¼ teaspoon salt
- ○ ¼ cup milk
- ○ 1 cup blueberries (pick your best cup from the Defrosting Berries experiment)
- ○ 1 quart-size (or larger) plastic baggie
- ○ Cooling rack
- ○ Butter knife

PROTOCOL:

1. Heat the oven to 425°F.

2. Rub the muffin pan with butter (or spray with nonstick cooking spray).

3. Mix the butter and sugar in a mixing bowl by hand (or with an electric mixer) until creamy. (This will be Mixing Bowl 1.)

4. Add the egg and stir.

5. Add the vanilla and stir.

6. In a medium bowl, stir together 1 cup of flour, baking powder, and salt.

7. Add half of the flour mixture to the butter and sugar mixture and stir.

8. Add 2 tablespoons of milk and stir.

9. Repeat steps 7–8.

10. Pour half of the batter into a second mixing bowl (Mixing Bowl 2).

EXPERIMENT A— NO FLOUR TOSS

PROTOCOL:

1. Add ½ cup of blueberries to Mixing Bowl 1 and gently stir.

2. Pour the batter into 3–4 muffin cups on one side of the muffin pan.
   PRO TIP: Using an ice cream scoop makes this step easier.

3. Use a few extra berries to label these muffins with an *A*.

EXPERIMENT B—FLOUR TOSS

PROTOCOL:

1. Add ½ cup of blueberries to the plastic baggie.

2. Add 2 tablespoons of flour to the baggie.

3. Gently toss the berries with flour. Make sure they are evenly coated.

4. Add the blueberries to Mixing Bowl 2 and gently stir.

5. Pour the batter into 3–4 muffin cups on the other side of the muffin pan.
   PRO TIP: Using an ice cream scoop makes this step easier.

6. Use a few extra berries to label these muffins with a *B*.

PROTOCOL (CONTINUED):

11. Bake the muffins for 5 minutes at 425°F.

12. Decrease the temperature to 375°F.

13. Bake for 20–25 more minutes (or until an inserted toothpick comes out clean).

14. Remove the muffins from the muffin pan and place them on a cooling rack.

15. Allow them to cool for 30 minutes.

16. Take one muffin from each experiment and slice it in half.

17. Analyze the appearance and location of the blueberries.

HOW IT WORKS:

Whoever convinced the world that we should eat muffins for breakfast deserves a gold medal! Traditionally speaking, a muffin has two distinct sections full of delicious molecules: (1) a bottom portion that is strong and sturdy, and (2) a dome-shaped top layer that is usually covered in sucrose (sugar). In this experiment, we used two different temperatures in order to make sure that both sections of the muffin were cooked perfectly. The higher temperature ensures that the sugar caramelizes on the top of the muffin, whereas the lower temperature takes care of the molecules in the base of the muffin.

The second thing we altered in this experiment was how we prepared the blueberries before adding them to the batter. In Experiment A, we added them directly to the batter, whereas in Experiment B, we coated them in flour first. Since flour is a hygroscopic material, it can easily absorb water from its surroundings. (This is why we keep our flour in airtight containers, otherwise it will absorb H_2O molecules from the atmosphere.) When we coat our berries in flour, the flour absorbs any of the extra juices that leak from the berries during the baking process. This is a good thing because this chemical reaction locks the berries into position within the muffin. Otherwise, the sticky juices will pull the berries down to the bottom of the pan, giving us an uneven berry distribution within the muffin (like we see in Experiment A).

SMOOTHIE

A Note from Kate: In summer 2019, Austin, Texas, had its second-hottest August on record, with 27 days of heat over 100°F. It was so hot that I started to make this morning smoothie as a way to escape from the heat. For this experiment, feel free to mix it up and use whatever frozen fruits you have in your freezer. I'm partial to strawberries and bananas, but some people prefer smoothies with pineapple or blueberries or any other fruit you can think of.

Messiness Level: 2/3

Materials:

○ Blender
○ 2 cups frozen strawberries, hulled
○ 1 fresh (or frozen) banana, peeled, broken into 3–4 pieces
○ ½ cup Greek yogurt
○ ½–¾ cup milk
○ 1–2 tablespoons chia seeds (optional)
○ A glass

Protocol:

1. Mix all of the ingredients together in the blender.

2. Blend until a homogenous mixture is formed.

3. Pour into a glass and examine the composition of the smoothie before testing it!

WHAT DO YOU THINK?

> Why do we use a blender to make the smoothie instead of an electric mixer or wooden spoon?
> Why do we use dairy products, like yogurt and milk, instead of just using water?
> What will happen if we use fresh strawberries instead of frozen strawberries?
> If you add chia seeds to the mixture, how does it change the chemistry of the beverage?

HOW It WORKS:

Fruits are primarily composed of polar water molecules, followed by fructose (sugar), some vitamins (vitamin C), and minerals (potassium). Strawberries have a very high water content at 92%, while bananas have a very low water content (74%). This is probably not too surprising since juice rarely shoots out of a banana when we eat it, but the same cannot be said for a strawberry.

On the other hand, Greek yogurt and milk are both dairy products, which means they contain lots of big fat molecules that have been dispersed within their watery base. The problem is, these large fat molecules are nonpolar and they do not mix easily with the polar water molecules found in the fruit. Therefore, in order for us to mix the watery juices from the strawberries and banana with the fatty molecules from the dairy products, we have to use a blender. With this incredible invention, the polar and nonpolar molecules can be mixed together to form an emulsion (a liquid trapped within a liquid) within a matter of minutes.

However, if you add chia seeds to the smoothie, then you actually make a completely different mixture called a colloid. This is where a solid is trapped within a liquid. If you look at your smoothie, you will see that the chia seeds are dispersed evenly throughout the smoothie. What you will not see is the seeds sitting at the bottom of the glass. Because of the way the seeds are scattered throughout the liquid, our smoothie is technically a colloid.

ACIDIC FRUIT

A NOTE FROM KATE: When I spend time at the beach, I like to pack healthy snacks in my cooler. One of my favorites is green apples with peanut butter, but I hate when the precut apples turn brown before I can eat them. That's why I created this experiment—with the hopes of getting to the bottom of which method is best for preserving my delicious precut apples.

MESSINESS LEVEL: 1/3

MATERIALS:

- 2 apples
- Knife
- 4 small bowls
- 2 lemons
- 1 cup orange juice
- 1 cup vinegar

PROTOCOL:

1. Ask an adult to help you cut the apples into 16 slices (8 slices per apple).

2. Place 4 apple slices into each bowl.

3. Label each bowl with numbers 1–4.

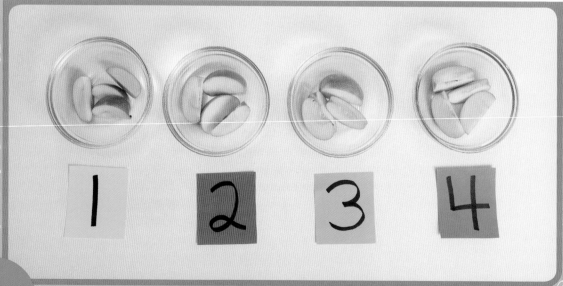

4. Analyze the apple slices in each bowl (and take a picture, if possible).

5. Cut the lemons in half. Squeeze the lemon juice over Bowl 1. (Don't worry about the seeds.)

6. Pour the orange juice over Bowl 2.

7. Pour the vinegar over Bowl 3.

8. Do nothing to Bowl 4.

9. After 5 minutes, examine the apples in each bowl, but do not touch them. We do not want to introduce any new variables into our experiment.

10. Continue to analyze the apples every 5–10 minutes for an hour (or more!).

11. When your observations are done, taste them!

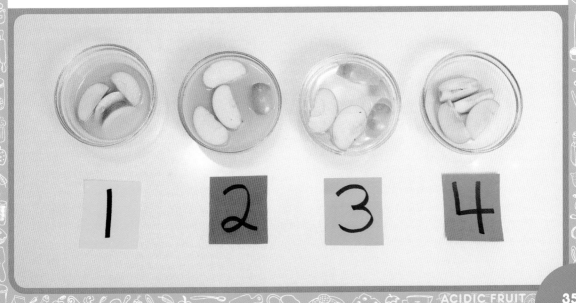

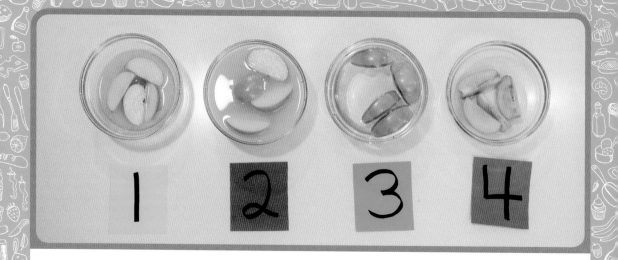

WHAT DO YOU THINK?

> Which apple turned brown the fastest? Why do you think that is?
> Which apple turned brown the slowest? Why do you think that is?
> What is one of the major disadvantages of using vinegar to prevent browning?
> What do you think would happen if you used a pear or an avocado instead of an apple?

HOW IT WORKS:

Lemons, oranges, and vinegar all have one thing in common: they all contain acids (molecules that have pH values lower than 7). Lemons and oranges contain an acid called citric acid, which is a big molecule with a pH of around 3. Lots of fruits contain citric acid, like pineapples and cherries, but it can also be found in many berries (e.g., strawberries, raspberries, blueberries). Most people don't know that citric acid can also be found in lots of our vegetables too, especially in tomatoes and broccoli, and even carrots! The only problem with using tomatoes (or broccoli) in our experiment is that our apples will be ruined after pouring tomato juice all over them.

On the other hand, I would rather have tomatoes and apples than vinegar and apples! Vinegar contains a different acid called acetic acid. Like citric acid, acetic acid has a pH lower than 7, but its pH is closer to 2. This means that acetic acid will work just as well as citric acid (maybe even better) to stop the browning from showing up on your apple.

The apples contain big molecules called enzymes that naturally occur within lots of fruits (and our bodies). Both citric and acetic acid react with these enzymes to slow down the process that causes browning on the insides of the apples. These enzymes struggle to complete the necessary chemical reactions in the acidic environments, so we can use lemons, orange juice, and even vinegar to keep the appetizing appearance of our precut apples.

DESERTED ISLAND CHALLENGE!

A NOTE FROM KATE: You have been stranded on a deserted island in the middle of the ocean. After wandering around for a few hours, you stumble upon a small container of camping gear and a box of the following items.

MESSINESS LEVEL: 2/3

MATERIALS:

- Mobile stove (you can use your regular stove)
- Skillet
- Saucepan
- Canned black beans
- Canned tomatoes
- Bag of rice
- Chicken broth
- Fresh water
- Olive oil
- A handful of spices

Using only one bonus item from your kitchen (and any fruit or veggie you can find on the island), how many different dishes can you create? I was able to come up with lots of different options, but here are my favorites. What about you?

MEAL 1: MANGO SALSA

Bonus item: Canned corn

Description: After spotting some mango on the island, I made a delicious mango black bean salsa with garlic salt, cumin, and onion powder.

MEAL 2: BEAN DIP

Bonus item: Shredded cheese
Description: With jalapeños found on the island, I concocted a spicy bean dip that would be perfect for any tropical party. For this recipe, I used garlic powder, cumin, chili powder, salt, and pepper.

MEAL 3: CHILI

Bonus item: Bell peppers
Description: By combining the chicken broth and tomatoes, I whipped up an incredible vegetarian chili. My spices were salt, pepper, oregano, cumin, paprika, chili powder, garlic powder, and onion powder.

MEAL 4: BEAN SOUP

Bonus item: Avocado
Description: Using avocado, I heated the black beans and chicken broth to make an easy black bean soup. For spices, I went with onion powder, garlic powder, chili powder, cumin, salt, and pepper.

MEAL 5: RISOTTO

Bonus item: Parmesan cheese
Description: The rice, chicken broth, tomatoes, and cheese can be combined to create a phenomenal risotto. I like to add a little bit of salt, pepper, and onion powder to round out the flavors.

MEAL 6: TOMATO SOUP

Bonus item: Breadsticks
Description: When we combine tomatoes with chicken broth (and some salt, pepper, onion powder, garlic powder, and thyme), we can produce a dazzling tomato soup. And I don't know about you, but I love to dip my breadsticks into the tomato soup!

MEAL 7: LEMON RICE

Bonus item: Heavy cream
Description: After finding a lemon tree on the island, I wanted to try my hand at making lemon rice by adding chicken broth, heavy cream, and rice. The lemon adds a little citric acid to give the dish its distinctive flavors, which are amplified with the addition of some dill or green onions (found on the north part of the island).

MEAL 8: PASTA SALAD

Bonus item: Pasta noodles

Description: This pasta salad was super easy to make! I used the black beans and tomatoes to make the salad, and the olive oil and spices to make the dressing. To top it off, I used a lime (found on the island, of course) to give the salad a zesty taste.

MEAL 9: RICE SALAD

Bonus item: Apple cider vinegar

Description: Using the rice, beans, and any peppers from the island, we can make a tasty rice salad. The apple cider vinegar–olive oil salad dressing is perfect for this dish, especially with some onion powder, garlic powder, and cumin.

MEAL 10: MEXICAN RICE

Bonus item: Fresh garlic

Description: My husband's family is Mexican, and they make the *best* rice dish (also called Spanish rice). All you need is rice, tomatoes, chicken broth, cumin, garlic, salt, and pepper. Now pair that with an island burrito to have the perfect snack.

HOW It WORKS:

Rice is a desiccant, which means that each grain will readily pull the moisture out of its environment. If you live in a humid area, this means that the rice will absorb the H_2O molecules from the air. The rice then becomes big and fluffy, and has a much softer texture.

This also happens any time we cook with rice. The rice absorbs the water (or chicken broth) and any of the surrounding flavors—that's why we add the salt and butter/oil to the water in the first few steps when making rice, instead of at the end.

PRO TIP: If you ever drop your cell phone in water, do not turn it on. Instead, put it in a plastic baggie with a cup of rice, and do not touch your phone for a week. Since the rice is hygroscopic, it will absorb all of the water molecules that are stuck in your phone!

BOUNCY BREAD BALLS

A NOTE FROM Kate: This experiment is wonderful for kinesthetic learners, people who learn best by doing things physically, because you have to really get your hands dirty and play with the dough! It's so much fun to stretch the dough, and to shape it into small bread balls to see if it will bounce. When you go through this experiment, make sure to stop and examine each type of dough. Is it stretchy? Can you bounce it? Channel your inner detective to figure out which dough produces the bounciest bread balls!

MESSINESS LEVEL: 3/3

MATERIALS (FOR EACH EXPERIMENT):

- ◯ 1½ cups water (ideally around 110°F)
- ◯ Small bowl
- ◯ 1 tablespoon sugar
- ◯ 2 teaspoons salt
- ◯ 0–2 tablespoons (up to 2 packets) of active dry yeast
- ◯ Dish towel
- ◯ 4 cups flour + more flour for kneading
- ◯ 1 tablespoon butter, melted
- ◯ 2 mixing bowls
- ◯ A warm place
- ◯ Oven
- ◯ Baking sheet
- ◯ Parchment paper or nonstick cooking spray or silicone baking mats
- ◯ Butter knife
- ◯ ¼ cup coarse salt

EXPERIMENT A—TWICE THE YEAST

PROTOCOL:

1. Put warm water in a small bowl. Be sure the water isn't hotter than 120°F or it will deactivate the yeast.

2. Add the sugar and salt. Stir the solution.

3. Add 4½ teaspoons (or 2 packets) of active dry yeast. It will sit on the top of the mixture.

4. Cover with a dish towel. Set aside for 5 minutes.

5. Stir together the flour and melted butter in a mixing bowl.

6. Slowly add the yeast mixture to the flour mixture and mix until a ball of dough forms.

7. Remove the dough from the bowl and knead by hand for 4–5 minutes (or use an electric mixer with a dough hook).

8. Pull on the dough a little bit. Is it stretchy? Make a few observations about the texture and appearance of the dough.

9. Put the dough in a lightly greased mixing bowl. Look at the size of the dough (if possible, take a picture).

10. Cover with the dish towel and store it in a warm place.

11. Check on the dough after 10 minutes. Has the size/shape of the dough changed?

12. Continue to check on the dough in 10-minute increments for a total of one hour. Be sure to record your observations in a notebook (or take pictures).

EXPERIMENT B—STANDARD YEAST

PROtOCOL:

1. Put warm water in a small bowl. Be sure the water isn't hotter than 120°F or it will deactivate the yeast.

2. Add the sugar and salt. Stir the solution.

3. Add 2¼ teaspoons (or 1 packet) of active dry yeast. It will sit on the top of the mixture.

4. Cover with a dish towel. Set aside for 5 minutes.

5. Stir together the flour and melted butter in a mixing bowl.

6. Slowly add the yeast mixture to the flour mixture and mix until a ball of dough forms.

7. Remove the dough from the bowl and knead by hand for 4–5 minutes (or use an electric mixer with a dough hook).

8. Pull on the dough a little bit. Is it stretchy? Make a few observations about the texture and appearance of the dough.

9. Put the dough in a lightly greased mixing bowl. Look at the size of the dough (if possible, take a picture).

10. Cover with the dish towel and store it in a warm place.

11. Check on the dough after 10 minutes. Has the size/shape of the dough changed?

12. Continue to check on the dough in 10-minute increments for a total of one hour. Be sure to record your observations in a notebook (or take pictures).

EXPERIMENT C—NO YEAST

PROTOCOL:

1. Stir the sugar, salt, and water together.

2. In a mixing bowl, stir together the flour and melted butter.

3. Slowly add the sugar mixture to the flour mixture and mix until a ball of dough forms.

4. Remove the dough from the bowl and knead by hand for 4–5 minutes (or use an electric mixer with a dough hook).

5. Pull on the dough a little bit. Is it stretchy? Make a few observations about the texture and appearance of the dough.

6. Put the dough in a lightly greased mixing bowl. Look at the size of the dough (if possible, take a picture).

7. Cover with the dish towel and store it in a warm place.

8. Check on the dough after 10 minutes. Has the size/shape of the dough changed?

9. Continue to check on the dough in 10-minute increments for a total of one hour. Be sure to record your observations in a notebook (or take pictures).

PROTOCOL (CONTINUED):

1. Heat the oven to 450°F.

2. Prepare a baking sheet (e.g., spray with nonstick cooking spray or line with parchment paper).

3. Remove the dough from Experiment A from the mixing bowl and analyze it. Is it stretchy? Make a few observations about the texture and appearance of the dough, and then roll it into long ropes.

4. Take one long rope and shape it into the letter *A*. Place it on the baking sheet.

5. Cut all of the other ropes into 1–1.5-inch pieces.

6. Roll each chunk of dough into a ball.

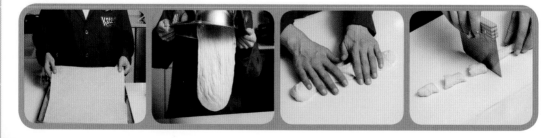

7. Place the bread balls next to the *A* on the baking sheet.

8. Sprinkle with coarse salt (optional).

9. Repeat steps 3–8 for the dough from Experiment B (except make a large *B* instead of the letter *A*).

10. Repeat steps 3–8 for the dough from Experiment C (except make a large *C* instead of the letters *A* or *B*).

11. Bake for about 12 minutes (or until golden brown).

12. Remove from the oven and inspect the appearance and texture of the three sets of bread balls.

WHAT DO YOU THINK?

> Why did we let the yeast sit in the water for 5 minutes before adding it to the flour?
> Compare the bread balls made from Experiments A, B, and C. What is different about their exteriors? Do they have the same overall appearance?
> Compare the interiors of the three sets of bread balls. Do they have the same consistency and texture?
> Which of the three doughs was the stretchiest?
> When we shaped the doughs into balls, which of the three was the bounciest?

HOW IT WORKS:

Our main variable in this experiment is the amount of yeast that we add in the very beginning. Experiment C, without any yeast, is our control. In chemistry experiments, we can use a control to compare against Experiments A and B to see the effect of adding yeast to our floury mixture. Since yeast is a fungus, it is commonly used as a leavening agent in baked goods. When a leavening agent is added to a dough, it releases lots of gas molecules, usually in the form of carbon dioxide. These bubbles are trapped within the dough, but they work together to try to escape. Macroscopically, using just our eyes, without any other tools, we can observe this over time when our dough increases in size. When yeast is used correctly, a traditional bread dough will double in size.

But how does that happen? The yeast reacts with the sucrose molecules in the sugar to produce two major products: carbon dioxide and ethanol. Both molecules push against the inside of the bread while they try to escape from the dough (once exposed to the heat from the oven). When this happens in Experiments A and B, we end up with big, fluffy, bouncy bread balls. This does not happen in Experiment C since we did not add any yeast to the dough.

BREADSTICKS

A Note From Kate: Ever since my sister worked at the Olive Garden in high school, I have been obsessed with the idea of making perfect at-home breadsticks. And even though I have never managed to decipher their secret recipe, I have a simple bread dough that is still pretty tasty. That's why I selected it for this investigation into how an egg wash affects the crust of baked bread. I hope you like it!

Messiness Level: 3/3

Materials:

- ○ 2 baking sheets
- ○ Parchment paper or nonstick cooking spray or silicone baking mats
- ○ 2 small bowls (or pourable containers)
- ○ 1¼ cups warm water (ideally around 110°F) + 1 tablespoon water
- ○ 2 tablespoons sugar
- ○ 2¼ teaspoons (or 1 packet) active dry yeast
- ○ Dish towel
- ○ Mixing bowl
- ○ 4 cups flour + more flour for kneading
- ○ 2 tablespoons butter, softened
- ○ 1 tablespoon salt
- ○ A warm place
- ○ Oven
- ○ 1 egg
- ○ Whisk or fork
- ○ Basting brush (or unused paintbrush or spoon)
- ○ ¼ cup coarse salt
- ○ Cooling rack

PROTOCOL:

1. Prepare baking sheets (spray with nonstick cooking spray or line with parchment paper or silicone baking mat).

2. Add the water and sugar to the small bowl and stir.

3. Slowly add the yeast to the top of the water.

4. Cover the bowl with a towel and set aside for 5 minutes.

5. To the mixing bowl, add the flour, butter, and salt.

6. Mix ingredients together with wooden spoon (or use an electric mixer).

7. Slowly add the yeast mixture to the flour mixture.

8. Stir for 5 minutes (or until a dough begins to form).

9. Gently knead the dough on a lightly floured surface for 2–3 minutes.

10. Divide the dough into roughly equal parts.

11. Roll each part into a long snake.

12. Divide each snake into 2-inch pieces.

13. Roll each 2-inch piece into a breadstick.

14. Place the breadsticks on the prepared baking sheets.

15. Cover the breadsticks with a towel and store in a warm place for 45–60 minutes (until the dough has doubled in size).

16. Heat the oven to 400°F.

17. Add 1 tablespoon of water and the egg to the empty small bowl.

18. Mix the egg and water together.

19. With the basting brush, gently cover the breadsticks on **one** baking sheet with the egg wash. Make sure to leave the other baking sheet as our control (without an egg wash).

20. If desired, sprinkle coarse salt over the breadsticks.

21. Bake the breadsticks for 8 minutes. Rotate the baking sheets 180° and bake for an additional 7 minutes (or until golden brown).

22. Once the breadsticks have finished baking, remove them from the oven.

23. Transfer to a rack to cool.

24. Compare the color/textures/tastes of the two different kinds of breadsticks.

WHAT DO YOU THINK?

> What was the primary difference between the appearance of the two types of breadsticks?
> If you close your eyes, can you determine which breadstick had the egg wash, just by the taste?
> What will happen if we break a breadstick in half? Can we snap the crust in half or do we have to use a ripping motion?
> What will happen to the color/finish of the breadstick if we wash it with just the egg yolk or just the egg white?

HOW IT WORKS:

Eggs are made of two small sacks of proteins, one called the egg white and one called the egg yolk. Egg whites start to turn into solids at around 63°C (145°F), but egg yolks can be heated up to 70°C (158°F). However, when the two sets of proteins are whisked together, new bonds are formed between the molecules that make the whisked egg more stable. This means that the mixture of an egg yolk and an egg white can be heated to around 73°C (165°F) before it will turn into a solid. For our experiment, the egg mixture will react with the molecules in the bread at even higher temperatures, which ultimately leads to the darkening of the outside of the bread.

But how does the egg wash change the *color* of the bread? First, the big protein molecules that exist in the eggs go through a chemical process called denaturation. During this process, the folded proteins open up—just like if they were to move from a tuck position to a snow angel position. After this, the proteins can coagulate, where they get really close together and form super-strong bonds. We can view the results of this microscopic reaction with our own eyes when we watch the breadsticks start to brown in the oven. The breadsticks with a thicker egg wash will end up with a darker color, so do your best to apply the egg wash evenly to each of your breadsticks!

PRETZEL BITES

A note from Kate: I've been working on my pretzel recipe for years, and I'm so excited to be finally sharing it with you. For this experiment, **make sure you are extra careful when working with the food-grade lye**. Always wear gloves, don't let the mixture touch your skin, and avoid using any silicone baking mats. And if you have time, pair this experiment with the Cheese Fondue for twice as much fun (and chemistry)!

Messiness Level: 3/3

Materials:

- 1½ cups (ideally around 110°F) + 20 cups water
- Small bowl
- 1 tablespoon sugar
- 2 teaspoons salt
- 2¼ teaspoons (or 1 packet) active dry yeast
- Dish towel
- 4 cups flour
- 1 tablespoon butter, melted
- 2 mixing bowls
- A warm place
- Oven
- Baking sheet
- Parchment paper or nonstick cooking spray
- Butter knife
- ¼ cup coarse salt
- ½ cup baking soda
- 2 large pots
- Tongs or spider strainer
- ¼ cup food-grade lye

Protocol:

1. Put warm water in a small bowl. Be sure the water isn't hotter than 120°F or it will deactivate the yeast.

2. Add the sugar and salt. Stir the solution.

3. Add active dry yeast. It will sit on the top of the mixture.

4. Cover with a dish towel. Set aside for 5 minutes.

5. Stir together the flour and melted butter in a mixing bowl.

6. Slowly add the yeast mixture to the flour mixture, and form a ball of dough.

7. Remove the dough from the bowl and knead by hand for 4–5 minutes (or use an electric mixer with a dough hook).

8. Put the dough in a lightly greased mixing bowl. Cover with the dish towel and store it in a warm place until the dough doubles in size (about an hour).

9. Heat the oven to 450°F.

10. Prepare a baking sheet (spray with nonstick cooking spray or line with parchment paper).

11. Remove the dough from the mixing bowl and roll into 3 long ropes.

12. Cut each rope into ten 1–1.5-inch pieces and roll each chunk of dough into a ball.

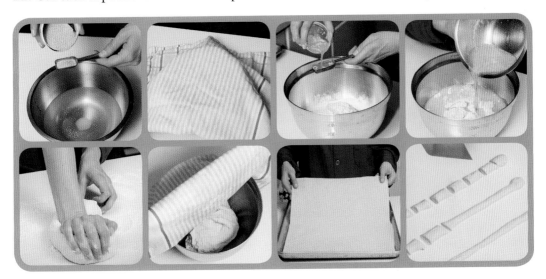

EXPERIMENT A—THE CONTROL

PROTOCOL:

1. Place 10 pretzel bites on a baking sheet.

2. Sprinkle with coarse salt.

3. Bake for about 12 minutes (or until golden brown).

4. Remove from the oven and inspect the appearance of the pretzels.

EXPERIMENT B—BAKING SODA

PROTOCOL:

1. Ask an adult to help you add ½ cup of baking soda into a large pot that contains 10 cups of water. Bring the mixture to a gentle boil.

2. **Carefully**, use tongs or a spider strainer to dip 10 pretzel bites into the pot for about 15 seconds, flip over, and then dip for another 15 seconds.

3. Remove the pretzel bites from the boiling mixture and place on a baking sheet.

4. Sprinkle with coarse salt.

5. Bake for about 12 minutes (or until golden brown).

6. Remove from the oven and inspect the appearance of the pretzels.

EXPERIMENT C—LYE (ADULT NEEDED)

PROTOCOL:

1. Put on gloves.

2. Ask an adult to help you add ¼ cup of food-grade lye into a large pot that contains 10 cups of water. Warm mixture on medium-low heat (no need to boil this solution).

3. **Carefully**, use tongs or a spider strainer to dip 10 pretzel bites into the pot for about 15 seconds, flip over, and dip for another 15 seconds. *Do not to touch the pretzels after they have been dipped in the lye!*

4. Remove the pretzel bites from the mixture and place on the baking sheet.

5. Remove gloves. Sprinkle pretzels with coarse salt.

6. Bake for about 12 minutes (or until golden brown).

7. Remove from the oven and inspect the appearance of the pretzels.
   DISPOSAL: After you are done with the lye, have an adult help you add water to the pot until it is full and then slowly pour it down the drain. Do not let the mixture touch your skin.

> Why did we have to complete Experiment A before moving on to Experiments B and C?
> Compare the pretzel bites made from Experiments A, B, and C. What is different about their exteriors?
> Smell each group of pretzel bites. Do they smell the same? Why or why not?
> What happens when we rip open each of the pretzel bites? Do their interiors look the same?
> Do the three types of pretzel bites taste the same? Why do you think that is?

HOW IT WORKS:

Baking soda and food-grade lye are both bases, which means they have a pH higher than 7. Baking soda is primarily composed of a molecule called sodium bicarbonate, and it has a pH of around 9. Sodium hydroxide, the main molecule found in food-grade lye, has a pH closer to 13 or 14. When we add the dough to a solution that contains a base, the outside of the dough turns a light yellow-brown color. This color change happens because the base breaks down the big protein molecules that are found in the flours of the dough. When this happens, the large molecules break into smaller molecules called amino acids. We have discovered over five hundred amino acids, and they each have their own unique structures.

These amino acids are very important in the browning reaction in pretzels. This chemical reaction, called the Maillard reaction, is what gives Bavarian pretzels their brown color and delicious flavor. Once the pretzels are in the oven (and exposed to heat), the small amino acids react with the sugar molecules (also found in the dough). Since baking soda is a weaker base than lye, the proteins in the flour don't react to the same degree as to the lye. This means that fewer amino acids will go through the Maillard reaction; therefore the baking soda pretzels are not quite as dark.

CHEESE FONDUE

A Note From Kate: The best cheese fondue I ever had was in Switzerland. We took a gondola to the top of a mountain and stuffed our faces with cheese and bread. It is one of my top 5 memories of studying abroad in Europe, and one of the main reasons why I repeatedly perform this experiment. I hope you like it as much as I do!

Messiness Level: 2/3

Materials–Experiment A–Preshredded Cheese:

- ⃝ Medium saucepan
- ⃝ ¾ cup preshredded Swiss cheese
- ⃝ 1 cup preshredded Gruyère cheese
- ⃝ ½ cup chicken broth
- ⃝ ¼ teaspoon lemon juice
- ⃝ 1½ teaspoons minced garlic
- ⃝ 1 tablespoon cornstarch
- ⃝ Gallon-size plastic baggie
- ⃝ ¼ teaspoon salt
- ⃝ ¼ teaspoon nutmeg
- ⃝ Pretzel Bites experiment from page 50, Breadsticks experiment from page 47, or any other crusty bread

Materials–Experiment B–Block Cheese:

- ⃝ Medium saucepan
- ⃝ Cheese grater
- ⃝ ¾ cup Swiss cheese, shredded from a block (at home)
- ⃝ 1 cup Gruyère cheese, shredded from a block (at home)
- ⃝ ½ cup chicken broth
- ⃝ ¼ teaspoon lemon juice
- ⃝ 1½ teaspoons minced garlic
- ⃝ 1 tablespoon cornstarch
- ⃝ Gallon-size plastic baggie
- ⃝ ¼ teaspoon salt
- ⃝ ¼ teaspoon nutmeg
- ⃝ Pretzels Bites experiment from page 50, Breadsticks experiment from page 47, or any other crusty bread

PROTOCOL:

1. Shred the cheeses for Experiment B.

2. Set up both saucepans (or fondue pots). Label the pans as Pan A and Pan B.

3. Add the chicken broth, lemon juice, and garlic to each saucepan.

4. Bring both saucepans to a simmer, then decrease the heat to medium-low.

5. Place both cheeses and the cornstarch for Experiment A in the plastic baggie (Bag A).

6. Shake the bag until all of the cheese has been covered in cornstarch.

7. Repeat steps 5–6 for Experiment B in a different plastic baggie (Bag B).

8. Add a handful of the cheese from Bag A to Pan A.

9. Gently stir the mixture and observe how the cheese melts.

10. Add a handful of the cheese from Bag B to Pan B.

11. Gently stir the mixture and observe how the cheese melts.

12. Repeat steps 8–11 until all of the cheese has been added to the pans.

13. After all the cheese has melted, add the spices to each pan and gently stir.

14. Use the breadsticks or pretzel bites to compare the taste and consistency of each fondue!

WHAT DO YOU THINK?

> Why did we coat the cheese in the cornstarch before adding it to the saucepan (or fondue pot)?
> Which cheese melted faster: the preshredded cheese or the block cheese? What about the Swiss cheese versus the Gruyère cheese?
> If you close your eyes, can you distinguish between the two fondues just by taste? What are the primary differences?
> Do the two fondues have the same final texture? Why or why not?

HOW IT WORKS:

There are over a thousand different types of cheeses that typically come from the milk of cows, goats, sheep, or buffalo. Since the milk is produced by different animals, each cheese has a unique taste and flavor derived from its ratio of proteins and fats. But regardless of the composition or animal origin, most cheeses are traditionally purchased as a solid dairy product, either in block or shredded form.

The block form of cheese is the purest version of cheese you can purchase. It is typically carved from a much larger block of cheese, and then wrapped tightly in a plastic casing. The cheese on the inside of the block is completely protected from the oxygen in the outside air, therefore it is nearly impossible for it to grow mold on the inside of the block cheese. The preshredded cheese, however, has much more surface area exposed to the air. In fact, all of the cheese that is on the inside of the baggie is completely exposed. This means that the manufacturer must also add preservatives to the cheese, in order to inhibit the growth of mold.

We can see the direct effect of the preservatives when we try to melt the two cheeses in this experiment. The preshredded cheese takes *much* longer than the block cheese to melt because of the added molecules (preservatives). Since these preservatives have been wrapped around the tiny shredded cheese pieces, it takes much more heat to break the bonds in the molecules of the preservatives. This is a problem for our fondue because this must happen before the preshredded cheese can melt. Ultimately, this is why the block cheese is a much better ingredient for the cheese fondue.

TOMATO SAUCE

A NOTE FROM KATE: This experiment is so much fun to do with a couple of friends. Make both sauces and see if your families can tell which one was made from fresh tomatoes. If you want to make it extra challenging, use a bandana as a blindfold to really test their palates!

MESSINESS LEVEL: 2/3

MATERIALS:

- ○ 2 onions
- ○ Knife
- ○ Cutting board
- ○ 2 saucepans
- ○ 2 cups fresh tomatoes, chopped (3 medium round tomatoes or 8 plum tomatoes)
- ○ 1 (16-ounce) can tomatoes with juices
- ○ Stove
- ○ 6 tablespoons butter
- ○ Wooden spoon
- ○ 1 teaspoon salt
- ○ ½ teaspoon pepper

PROTOCOL:

1. Peel the onions and ask an adult to help you cut them in half.

2. Place one onion (two halves) in Saucepan 1 and the other onion in Saucepan 2.

3. Ask an adult to help you chop up the fresh tomatoes.

4. Add the chopped tomatoes to Saucepan 1.

5. Open the can of tomatoes and pour the juices into Saucepan 2.

6. Chop up the canned tomatoes (if they are not already chopped) and add them to Saucepan 2.

7. Heat both saucepans over medium heat.

8. Add 3 tablespoons of butter to each saucepan and stir.

9. Add ½ teaspoon of salt to each saucepan and stir.

10. Add ¼ teaspoon of pepper to each saucepan and stir.

11. Continue to heat both saucepans over medium heat until they simmer.

12. Cook for 45 minutes, stirring occasionally.

13. Remove the pans from the heat.

14. Examine each sauce. Be sure to take note of the color, thickness, smell, and taste.

HOW IT WORKS:

Believe it or not, tomatoes are technically a berry that comes from a plant called *Solanum lycopersicum*. And just like with other berries, when you slice a tomato in half, you will be able to see its seeds. However, since tomatoes are not as sweet as most other fruits (like strawberries or apples), they are considered to be a culinary vegetable. This means that you are much more likely to eat tomatoes with your entrée, instead of your dessert.

The tomato sauces that we made in this experiment taste relatively similar. That's because canned tomatoes are really just tomatoes that have been removed from the vine of a tomato plant and then put into very hot water. When the tomato experiences the thermal energy from the hot water, the molecules in the skin move around quickly and pull away from the insides of the tomato (making them easy to remove). The peeled tomatoes are then put directly into the can. From here, the manufacturers can add more tomato juice and spices, but otherwise, canned tomatoes are really just tomatoes that someone else peeled for you.

A common misconception about canned tomatoes is that manufacturers add preservatives (molecules that prevent bacteria growth) to the can. While we do not want bacteria to grow in our can, we do not need to add any extra molecules because tomatoes act like their own preservatives! Tomatoes are naturally acidic (pH less than 7), and bacteria cannot grow in that environment. So canned tomatoes should really taste very similar to fresh tomatoes, which is why our tomato sauces should have the same flavors too.

RAINBOW PASTA

A NOTE FROM KATE: After finishing my tomato sauce experiment, I wanted to find a way to use the sauces. I had just restocked the pantry, so I decided to make some fresh pasta using 3 different types of flour. Feel free to use your science skills and experiment with whatever flour you have in your pantry—I just used three flours I had in mine.

MESSINESS LEVEL: 3/3

MATERIALS:

- ○ 9 eggs
- ○ Small bowl
- ○ Whisk
- ○ 2 cups all-purpose flour
- ○ 2¼ teaspoons + 1–2 tablespoons salt
- ○ Mixing bowl
- ○ 3 tablespoons olive oil
- ○ 1½ teaspoons food coloring
  (3 different colors; optional)
- ○ Plastic wrap
- ○ 2 cups cake flour
- ○ 2 cups whole wheat flour
- ○ Rolling pin
- ○ Knife
- ○ Water
- ○ Large pot
- ○ Stove
- ○ Spider strainer

PROTOCOL:

1. Crack 3 eggs into the small bowl.

2. Use the whisk to gently beat the 3 eggs into a homogenous mixture, so it all looks the same. Set aside.

3. Add the all-purpose flour and ¾ teaspoon salt to the mixing bowl and stir (or use an electric mixer with the hook attachment).

4. Add the egg mixture, 1 tablespoon oil, and ½ teaspoon of food coloring (in the first color, if using different colors) to the flour mixture and stir.

5. Knead the dough by hand until it is one cohesive ball of dough (or use an electric mixer for about 2–4 minutes).
   PRO TIP: If your dough feels dry, add ⅛ teaspoon of water and stir. Repeat until the dough sticks together.

6. Wrap the dough in plastic wrap. If you are not using food coloring, label the dough as Experiment A. Set aside for 30 minutes. If you are using food coloring, record which color you used for Experiment A.

7. While the dough is resting, crack 3 more eggs, then use the whisk to gently beat the 3 eggs into a homogenous mixture in the small bowl. Set aside.

8. Add the cake flour and ¾ teaspoon salt to medium bowl and stir.

9. Repeat steps 4–6 (using a different color for the dough).

PROTOCOL (CONTINUED):

10. Wrap the dough in plastic wrap, label as Experiment B (or record which color was used for Experiment B), and set aside for 30 minutes.

11. While the second dough is resting, crack 3 more eggs, then use the whisk to gently beat the 3 eggs into a homogenous mixture in the small bowl. Set aside.

12. Add the whole wheat flour and ¾ teaspoon salt to medium bowl and stir.

13. Repeat steps 4–6 (using a different color for this dough too).

14. Wrap the dough in plastic wrap, label as Experiment C (or record which color was used), and set aside for 30 minutes.

15. At this time, the dough for Experiment A should be ready. Remove the plastic wrap and use a rolling pin to roll out the dough. Try to make it as thin as possible.

16. Ask a parent to help you cut the dough into your desired shape (e.g., long, skinny fettuccini; thicker pappardelle; butterfly-shaped farfalle; or hand-torn strapponi).

17. Repeat steps 15–16 with the doughs made from Experiments B and C.
    PRO TIP: In order to minimize variables in your experiment, try to be consistent with the thickness of your dough. It's also a good idea to use the same shape of pasta too.

18. If you have a drying rack, you can hang your pasta to dry for the best consistency. (If not, it'll still taste good.)

19. Fill the large pot ⅔ full with water. Add the salt and bring the mixture to a boil.

20. Add the pasta from Experiments A, B, and C to the water and cook for 2–5 minutes (or until the pasta is al dente). Cook the three batches of pasta separately if you didn't use food coloring.

21. Use the spider strainer to remove the pasta from the water.

22. Compare the color, texture, and taste of the different pasta noodles.

23. Add the Tomato Sauce you made from the experiment on page 59, or your favorite sauce, and stir. Enjoy your rainbow pasta!

WHAT DO YOU THINK?

> Which pasta dough was the most difficult to form into a ball? Why do you think that is?
> What happened during the resting phase? Did the dough change in shape or size?
> Which flour made the best-tasting pasta? What about best-looking pasta?
> What would happen if we added gelatin to the dough instead of food coloring?

HOW It WORKS:

In this experiment, we tested the difference between using three types of flours when making homemade pasta. The three flours that I used (although you may have used other ones) were all-purpose, cake, and whole wheat. All-purpose flours (and whole wheats) are considered to be hard flours because they are made from hard wheat berries that have high protein levels. Proteins are large molecules called polypeptides, which means they have been built from two or more amino acids. But cake flour is actually classified as a soft flour because it is derived from soft wheat berries that are softer and shorter than hard wheat berries. Both of these factors contribute to the lower protein concentration in soft flours.

Regardless of the hard or soft properties, all wheat is composed of three key pieces. The majority of the wheat berry is called the endosperm, and it is the part that contains most of the proteins. A much smaller section of the grain, the germ, is stuffed with vitamins and minerals (and a few more protein molecules). Lastly, we have the bran, which is the outer layer of the kernel, and that is where we get our fiber.

During the manufacturing process, the endosperm is separated from the other parts of the wheat to form a white flour (like our all-purpose and cake flours). If the germ is left in the flour, the two parts combine to form our brown flours. Whole wheat flours are made from all three parts, which is why they are typically considered to be the healthiest of the three flours. However, as we can see from our experiment, the healthiest flour does not always make the best pasta dough. Instead, that honor is usually earned by softer flours, like cake flour and Italian 00 flour. As you probably know from eating pasta for dinner, their lower protein contents give the pasta its classic "chewy" texture.

STIR-FRIED PEPPERS

A NOTE FROM Kate: In order to make the peppers, we first have to test the smoke point of four different fats and oils. I love this experiment because it is excellent for practicing your basic scientific skills—like coming up with a hypothesis. So, what do you think? Which fat/oil will be able to resist the most heat: canola oil, peanut oil, clarified butter, or butter? Once you've made your prediction, grab an adult and get started on the experiment. **Make sure you are extra careful with this one**—I don't want you accidentally starting a grease fire!

Messiness Level: 3/3

Materials:

- ○ Skillet + lid
- ○ Stove
- ○ 1 tablespoon canola (or vegetable) oil
- ○ Kitchen timer (or stopwatch)
- ○ 1 tablespoon peanut oil
- ○ 1 tablespoon butter
- ○ 1 tablespoon clarified butter (like ghee)
- ○ 3 bell peppers
- ○ 1 jalapeño (optional)
- ○ Knife
- ○ Cutting board
- ○ Heat-safe spatula (or wooden spoon)
- ○ 1–2 teaspoons salt (to taste)
- ○ ¼ teaspoon pepper (to taste)
- ○ ½ teaspoon garlic powder (to taste)
- ○ ¾ teaspoon chili powder (to taste)

PROTOCOL:

1. Heat your skillet over medium-high heat for 5 minutes.

2. Add the canola or vegetable oil to the center of the pan and start your timer.
   PRO TIP: Be ready to turn on your exhaust fan as soon as you see the smoke point.

3. Record the amount of time it takes until the oil starts to smoke. Turn off the heat completely and record the smoking point of the canola or vegetable oil (the time it took for the oil to begin to smoke).

4. After the pan has **completely cooled**, rinse it off and put it back on the stove (or use a clean skillet if one's available).

5. Repeat steps 1–4 for peanut oil, butter, and clarified butter.

6. Compare your results to determine which fat/oil has the highest smoke point (takes the longest to start smoking). Use this fat/oil for the rest of the experiment.

7. Heat your skillet for one minute less than the amount of time it took to reach the smoking point.

8. While the pan is heating, cut the peppers into ¾-inch strips.

9. Add 2 tablespoons of your selected fat/oil (mine is clarified butter) to the center of the pan and use the spatula to spread it across the bottom of the pan.

10. **Have a parent help you** add the peppers to the pan.

11. Use the heat-safe spatula to turn the peppers in the fat/oil.

12. Heat the peppers until their skins start to brown.

13. Remove the pan from the heat.

14. Add salt, pepper, garlic powder, and chili powder.

15. Stir the peppers and the seasoning for about one minute in the hot pan.

16. Cover the pan for 30–60 seconds.

17. Remove the lid and stir.

18. Enjoy your peppers!

WHAT DO YOU THINK?

> What is the major difference between the fats and the oils?
> Did you notice a difference in the way the solids and liquids reacted to the heat?
> Which fat or oil had the highest smoke point?
> What would happen if we prepared the bell peppers with the fat or oil that has the lowest smoke point?

HOW It WORKS:

Once we've heated our pan, we add the fats and oils. While fats and oils come from the same category of molecules (triglycerides), fats are always in the solid phase and oils are always in the liquid phase. That's why butter is considered to be a fat and canola oil is considered to be, well, an oil. At the molecular level, there is one major difference between the fats and oils too. Oils, like olive oil and avocado oil, always have at least one double bond between two of their carbon atoms. We call this type of triglyceride an unsaturated fat. Butter, on the other hand, does not have any double bonds and we call this type a saturated fat. These molecules have a unique tubular shape that allows them to pack closely together, and are one of the main reasons why butter is a solid at room temperature.

Each of the fats/oils in our experiment had a completely different smoke point because they were each made from very different starting materials. For example, the canola oil (from rapeseed) has a smoke point of 400°F compared to peanut oil's (from peanuts) smoke point of 450°F. However, if we refine (or purify) the solution, then the fat/oil will have an even higher smoke point. That's because heat causes the molecules in the mixtures to decompose, and the impurities in unrefined fats/oils break down at lower temperatures.

We were able to observe this difference in smoke point when we compared butter to clarified butter. Since the clarified butter does not have the extra water and milk solids (and is therefore more pure than butter), it has a much higher smoke point of 482°F compared to butter's smoke point of 302°F. Interestingly, clarified butter is actually made by heating regular butter and pulling the butterfat out of the mixture (that contains water and milk solids). This butterfat is what we call clarified butter.

CARAMEL CANDIES

A NOTE FROM KATE: This experiment happens quickly, so I highly recommend gathering all of the ingredients before you get started. Also, be careful when you add the melted butter solution to the sugar in step 13—sugar bubbles try to jump out of the pan and they are **hot**. Make sure to grab an adult to help you with this step.

MESSINESS LEVEL: 2/3

MATERIALS:

- ½ cup butter
- Small microwave-safe bowl
- Oil
- 9x5-inch bread pan or any deep plastic food container
- Parchment paper (11x7 inches)
- ¼ cup light corn syrup
- 2 tablespoons water
- Small saucepan with lid
- Butter knife or chopstick
- 1 cup sugar
- Stove
- ¾ cup heavy cream
- Microwave
- Coarse salt (optional)

PROTOCOL:

1. Take the butter out of the fridge and cut it into 6–8 small pieces. Put it in the small bowl and set aside.

2. Oil the inside of the bread pan.

3. Cut a piece of parchment paper to line the inside of the bread pan (about 11x 7 inches).

4. Place the parchment paper in the pan and lightly coat with oil. Set aside.

PROTOCOL (CONTINUED):

5. Put the corn syrup and water into a small saucepan and stir with a butter knife or chopstick (or any heat-resistant long, thin item that is not a spoon).

6. Slowly add the sugar to the mixture. Do your best to try not to get any sugar on the sides of the saucepan.

7. Gently stir the solution with the butter knife.

8. Bring the mixture to a boil over medium heat. Continue to gently stir while the mixture heats up.

9. Cover with a lid for 60 seconds.

10. Remove the lid and let the sugar mixture heat undisturbed for the next 5–10 minutes until the mixture turns a light amber color (do not stir it).

11. While the sugar solution is heating, add the heavy cream to the butter in the small bowl.

12. Heat the butter and cream in the microwave until the butter has completely melted (about 60 seconds).

13. As soon as the sugar mixture turns a light amber color, **ask a parent to help you** add about 15% of the melted butter solution (approximately 3 tablespoons).
CAUTION: When you add the cream/butter solution, the hot sugar solution will bubble up quickly. Be careful!

14. Stir with the butter knife.

15. Repeat steps 13–14 until all of the cream/butter solution has been added to the sugar mixture.

16. Heat the mixture for 5–10 more minutes. If you want soft caramels, remove the pan from the heat after 5 minutes. If you want harder caramels, wait the full 10 minutes.

17. Pour the mixture into the parchment-lined bread pan.

18. Cool for 30 minutes. Sprinkle with coarse salt if you want a sweet-and-salty treat (optional).

19. Cool for 3 more hours (or until the caramels have hardened).

20. Ask a parent to help you cut the caramels into your caramel candy shape. Most people do 1-inch cubes or 1x1.5-inch rectangles, but I think it's fun to try to make stars and circles too.

21. Don't forget to taste test your final product!
    CLEANING TIP: Have an adult help you boil water in your caramel pans after you are done with the experiment. The caramel will dissolve in the hot water, which will make the cleanup process much easier.

WHAT DO YOU THINK?

› Why did we oil the pan before adding the parchment paper?
› Why did we put the butter and heavy cream into the microwave?
› What will happen if we double the amount of sugar or heavy cream?
› What will happen if we use dark corn syrup or brown sugar?

HOW IT WORKS:

Table sugar is a disaccharide molecule called sucrose. It is not as sweet as the sugars found in most fruits (fructose), but is definitely sweeter than the sugars found in most vegetables (glucose). If you're wondering why an apple, with fructose in it, is not as sweet as a caramel candy, it's because of the concentration of sugar in each item—there's a *lot* more sucrose in caramel than there is fructose in an apple. What I love about sucrose is that it is produced when one glucose molecule reacts with one fructose molecule. That's why it's called a disaccharide, which literally means *two sugars* (in Latin, *di* = two and *saccharide* = sugar).

When table sugar is heated to make a caramel sauce, the white solid slowly converts into a thick yellow liquid before ultimately turning into a darker brown substance. This process is called caramelization, and it is usually characterized by its change in color and an incredible array of smells. The caramel actually forms when the final brown liquid hardens, which occurs *after* all of the fragrant compounds have been released into the atmosphere.

Microscopically, the caramel forms when the sugar decomposes. When sucrose interacts with heat, its bonds break to form glucose and fructose, two monosaccharides or single sugars (*mono* = one). This mixture of molecules is the yellow liquid that we see. From there, glucose and fructose continue to break apart into hundreds of different smaller molecules—some sweet, some bitter, some very fragrant—which is why we can usually smell when the caramels are ready to be removed from the stove.

CHOCOLATE-COVERED PRETZELS

A Note From Kate: My sister and I were fortunate enough to grow up with another set of sisters who were our close friends. We were always at each other's houses, and loved coming up with different projects to fill our time. Every winter, we would get together and make a ridiculous number of Chocolate-Covered Pretzels. I was inspired by our goofy pretzel concoctions when deriving this experiment. So, I would like to dedicate this experiment to my muses: Katie, Becky, and Brittany.

Messiness Level: 3/3

Materials:

- ○ Baking sheet
- ○ Parchment paper (or nonstick cooking spray or silicone baking mat)
- ○ 4 ounces white baking chocolate
- ○ 4 small microwave-safe bowls
- ○ 4 tablespoons vegetable shortening
- ○ Microwave
- ○ 1 bag of pretzel rods
- ○ 4 ounces unsweetened baking chocolate (100% cacao)
- ○ 4 ounces semi-sweet baking chocolate (56% cacao)
- ○ 4 ounces milk chocolate baking chocolate (32% cacao)
- ○ Refrigerator

PROTOCOL:

1. Prepare a baking sheet (spray with nonstick cooking spray or line with parchment paper or silicone baking mat).

2. Break up the white chocolate into small, bite-size pieces.

3. Place it into Bowl 1.

4. Add 1 tablespoon of vegetable shortening to Bowl 1.

5. Microwave Bowl 1 for 30 seconds.

6. Remove from the microwave. Analyze the appearance of the chocolate and then stir.

7. Continue to microwave the chocolate in 10-second increments (stirring after each session) until all of the chocolate has melted. Record your observations.

8. Dip the pretzel rod into the melted chocolate and rotate to coat evenly.
   PRO TIP: Use a basting brush to brush the chocolate onto the pretzel for more even coverage.

9. Place the pretzel on the baking sheet.

10. Repeat steps 8–9 for four more pretzel rods.
    MINI-EXPERIMENT: Consider brushing the salt off one of the pretzels before dipping it in chocolate. You can compare the way the chocolate sticks to the unsalted pretzel versus the ones with salt.

11. Repeat steps 2–10 for each of the other chocolates. Do your best to break up each of the chocolates into similar-size pieces. Make sure to record the total time it takes for each chocolate to melt, and describe the final appearance of each chocolate on the pretzels.

12. Place the baking sheet in the refrigerator for 20–30 minutes (until all of the chocolate has solidified).

13. Compare the final products and then share your Chocolate-Covered Pretzels with your friends and family!

WHAT DO YOU THINK?

> Were you surprised by how long it took for each chocolate to melt?
> Which chocolate melted the most evenly? What about the fastest?
> After the chocolate solidified, did all of the pretzels look the same?
  Why or why not?
> Did the amount of salt crystals on the pretzel affect the way the chocolate clung
  to the pretzel? Why or why not?

HOW IT WORKS:

Vegetable shortening is made of triglyceride molecules that exist in the solid phase. The term *shortening* is a generic term that can be used for any type of fat that exists as a solid at room temperature. It first earned its name back in the nineteenth century, when it was used to shorten dough. The shortening disrupted the bonds within the dough, which made the resulting baked goods taste light and flaky.

Vegetable shortening is a specific type of shortening that is made from vegetable oil. Traditionally, vegetable oil is made of triglyceride molecules that have one double bond. However, manufacturers can hydrogenate vegetable oil—basically, they add hydrogen to it—which converts that double bond into a single bond. When this happens, the vegetable *oil* turns into vegetable *shortening* (fat), which is a much better ingredient for pies.

When the vegetable shortening starts to melt in the microwave, the surrounding chocolate melts too. Lighter chocolates (like white chocolate and milk chocolates) melt at lower temperatures, around 40–45°C (104–113°F), whereas darker chocolates melt at higher temperatures, around 45–50°C (113–122°F). These melting points are a direct result of how much cocoa is in the original chocolate. The more cocoa a chocolate has, the higher its melting point will be.

DRAGON CUPCAKES

A NOTE FROM KATE: My Dragon Cupcakes with Dragon Frosting are so bright and colorful that they can turn any day around. So, if your friend is having a bad day, invite them over to bake some Dragon Cupcakes—you can't go wrong with this experiment!

MESSINESS LEVEL: 3/3

MATERIALS:

- ○ 2 tablespoons + ¼ cup butter, softened
- ○ Oven
- ○ Muffin pan
- ○ Nonstick cooking spray
- ○ 2 teaspoons + ½ cup flour
- ○ 1–2 teaspoons clarified butter (or coconut oil)
- ○ 1 cupcake liner
- ○ ⅔ cup white sugar
- ○ Mixing bowl
- ○ 2 eggs
- ○ 3 teaspoons vanilla
- ○ Medium bowl
- ○ 1 cup + 2 teaspoons flour
- ○ 1 teaspoon baking powder
- ○ ½ teaspoon salt
- ○ ½ cup milk
- ○ ½ cup measuring cup (or ice cream scoop)
- ○ Food coloring (variety of colors)
- ○ Butter knife
- ○ Cooling rack

PROtoCOL:

1. Take the butter out of the refrigerator and set aside.

2. Heat the oven to 350°F.

3. Spray the muffin cup in the upper-left corner of the muffin pan with nonstick cooking spray. This is Cupcake 1.

4. Use 1 tablespoon of butter to coat the muffin cup to the right of Cupcake 1. This is Cupcake 2.

5. Use 1 tablespoon of butter to coat the muffin cup below Cupcake 1. This is Cupcake 3.

6. Add 1 teaspoon of flour to cover the butter in Cupcake 3 (*not* Cupcake 2).

7. Use the clarified butter (or coconut oil) to coat the muffin cup to the right of Cupcake 3. This is Cupcake 4.

8. Add 1 teaspoon of flour to cover the clarified butter in Cupcake 4.

9. Add the cupcake liner to the muffin cup below Cupcake 3. This is Cupcake 5.

10. The empty muffin cup to the right of Cupcake 5 is our "control cupcake," and it is intentionally left bare. This is Cupcake 6.

11. Cream together the butter (¼ cup) and sugar in a mixing bowl by hand (or with an electric mixer).

12. Add the eggs and stir.

13. Add the vanilla and stir.

14. In a medium bowl, stir together ½ cup flour, baking powder, and salt.

15. Add half of the flour mixture to the butter and sugar mixture and stir.

16. Add 2 tablespoons of milk and stir.

17. Repeat steps 15–16.

18. Split the cupcake batter into the 6 prepared muffin cups, pouring ½ cup of cupcake batter into each muffin cup. PRO TIP: Using an ice cream scoop makes this step easier.

19. Use 5–6 drops of food coloring to label each cupcake. Use a butter knife to gently mix in the color. Here's an example of what you could do:

POSITION, EXPERIMENT, COLOR
CUPCAKE 1: Nonstick spray, purple
CUPCAKE 2: Butter, blue
CUPCAKE 3: Butter + flour, green
CUPCAKE 4: Clarified butter + flour, red
CUPCAKE 5: Cupcake liner, orange
CUPCAKE 6: Nothing, yellow

20. Bake 16–18 minutes (or until an inserted toothpick comes out clean).

21. Ask an adult to help you carefully remove each cupcake from the muffin pan. Pay attention to how hard/easy it is to remove each one from the pan. Be sure to take a minute to observe the bottom of each cupcake and the appearance of the corresponding muffin cup.

22. Place each cupcake on a cooling rack.

23. Allow them to cool completely.

24. If you are feeling creative, decorate the cupcakes with Dragon Frosting (the next experiment in this book).

WHAT DO YOU THINK?

› Which cupcake was the easiest to remove from the muffin pan? Why do you think that was?
› Were there any cupcakes that were more difficult to remove from the muffin pan than the control (Cupcake 6)?
› Which cupcake color was the brightest? Did the color fade after baking the cupcakes in the oven?
› Did the nonstick cooking spray, butter, or clarified butter affect the taste of the cupcake?

HOW IT WORKS:

In many of the experiments in this book, I ask you to use a nonstick cooking spray, butter, or parchment paper to cover the metal surface on something like a muffin pan. All of these items are generally used to provide a thin line of protection between the baked good and the baking sheet, and in this experiment we actually get to investigate how that works.

In Cupcakes 1–4, we examined four different triglycerides, which is a fancy word for oils or fats. When triglycerides are in the solid phase, we call them fats (like butter). When they are in the liquid phase, we call them oils (like olive oil). Both oils and fats are nonpolar molecules, which means that they do not want to mix with polar molecules (like the water in our cupcake batter).

In Cupcake 1, we used a cooking spray that uses tiny liquid droplets of oil to stick to the muffin cup. These nonpolar molecules repel the cupcake batter, which helps to keep the cupcake from sticking to the pan. Cupcakes 2–3 use butter in the same way, but we added a little extra flour to Cupcake 3. This flour absorbs the very top layer of butter to prevent the cupcake from absorbing the grease. While this shouldn't change the way the cupcake sticks to the muffin cup (although lots of times it does), it will always change the oiliness of the bottom of the cupcake. Cupcake 4 is a mixture of Cupcakes 1 and 3, and if you used coconut oil, it just has a little extra coconut flavor! Cupcake 5 has a physical barrier between the muffin pan and the cupcake— the only problem is that the cupcake is now stuck to the cupcake liner! Once you've done this experiment, you can choose your favorite nonstick method for your future batches of Dragon Cupcakes.

DRAGON FROSTING

A NOTE FROM Kate: I love to make cupcakes, but I never have the patience to decorate them. That's why I am obsessed with this easy-peasy buttercream frosting experiment. It's quick, it's simple, and most importantly, it's absolutely delicious. When I'm feeling creative, I combine my food colorings to come up with neat hues, like teal and aqua. But now it's your turn. Which wild color combinations can you come up with?

Messiness Level: 3/3

Materials:

- ○ ½ cup butter
- ○ 4 ounces cream cheese
- ○ 2 mixing bowls
- ○ 2 cups powdered sugar
- ○ 1 teaspoon vanilla
- ○ 2 tablespoons whole milk
  (or any other milk)
- ○ 3–4 drops food coloring
  (2 different colors)
- ○ 2 quart-size plastic baggies

PROTOCOL:

1. Remove the butter and cream cheese from the fridge and allow them to warm to room temperature.

2. Mix the butter and sugar in a mixing bowl by hand (or with an electric mixer) until creamy.

3. Add ½ cup of the powdered sugar and stir.

4. Repeat step 3 until you have added all the powdered sugar.

5. Add the vanilla and stir.

6. Remove half of the frosting and place into a second mixing bowl (Mixing Bowl 2).

7. To Mixing Bowl 1, add the milk and stir for 3 minutes by hand (or with an electric mixer).

8. To Mixing Bowl 2, add the cream cheese and stir for 3 minutes by hand (or with an electric mixer).

9. Add 3–4 drops (or more) of food coloring to each bowl and stir. Use one color for Mixing Bowl 1 and another color for Mixing Bowl 2. Record which color you assigned to each mixing bowl.

10. Stir for 30–60 seconds longer (until the color of the frosting is smooth and homogenous).

11. Scoop each frosting into its own baggie.

12. Cut 1 inch off the bottom left corner off each plastic baggie.

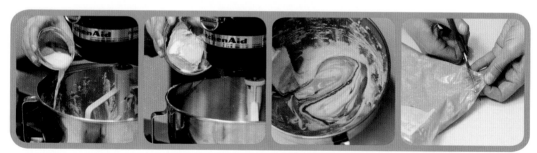

13. Squeeze the baggie to force the frosting out of the precut corner and apply to your favorite cupcakes.
PRO TIP: Make sure your cupcakes are completely cool before adding the frosting.

14. Have your friends, parents, and siblings do a blind taste test to determine which is the better frosting!

WHAT DO YOU THINK?

› What would happen if we used white or brown sugar instead of powdered sugar?
› What would happen if we used heavy cream instead of milk?
› What was the major difference between the appearance and texture of the two frostings?
› Did the two frostings taste the same? Was one sweeter than the other?

HOW IT WORKS:

Powdered sugar is made up of lots of sucrose molecules, just like granular sugar. The major difference is that powdered sugar has been ground up into extremely tiny pieces that make it look like a "powder." When the molecules are in this state, they readily absorb water from the atmosphere. For that reason, the powdered sugar is spiked with an additive to prevent clumping. Most manufacturers just add cornstarch, but sometimes potato starch is used too.

Cornstarch and potato starch are called anticaking agents. These molecules are very unique because they readily form bonds with water. When this happens, it prevents the water molecules from forming bonds with anything else in their vicinity (like the powdered sugar), which keeps the powdered sugar in our kitchen cabinet free of clumps. In our experiment, the anticaking agents keep the frosting nice and smooth, which prevents it from having a lumpy (or granular) texture.

The frosting made from the cream cheese was very similar to the traditional buttercream frosting. However, the main difference is that we swapped the milk for the cream cheese. Both the milk and cream cheese provide the frosting with the necessary fats to maintain the creamy texture of a classic buttercream frosting. However, if you completed this experiment with low-fat milk or skim milk, I highly recommend that you try it again with whole milk. I guarantee you will end up with a much thicker frosting!

UNICORN SUGAR COOKIES

A Note From Kate: For this experiment, I decided to use a simple sugar cookie to investigate the effect of white sugar, brown sugar, and dark brown sugar in a cookie. Since white sugar and brown sugar have different compositions, it's important that you remember to pack the brown sugar (if you do not have access to a scale). More importantly, make sure to slowly taste each of your final products to determine which cookie sweetener is your favorite!

Messiness Level: 2/3

Materials (For Each Experiment):

○ 1 cup unsalted butter, softened
○ Oven
○ Baking sheet
○ Parchment paper or nonstick cooking spray or silicone baking mat
○ Sugar:
　EXPERIMENT A—WHITE SUGAR: 1½ cups white sugar
　EXPERIMENT B—LIGHT BROWN SUGAR: 1½ cups light brown sugar
　EXPERIMENT C—DARK BROWN SUGAR: 1½ cups dark brown sugar
○ Mixing bowl
○ Wooden spoon
○ 1 egg
○ 1 teaspoon vanilla
○ ½ teaspoon food coloring
○ 3 cups flour
○ ¾ teaspoon baking powder
○ ¼ teaspoon salt
○ Big spoon
○ Cooling rack

PROTOCOL:

1. Remove the butter from the refrigerator and set aside to soften.

2. Heat the oven to 375°F.

3. Prepare a baking sheet (spray with nonstick cooking spray or line with parchment paper or silicone baking mat).

4. Mix the butter and sugar for Experiment A in a mixing bowl with a wooden spoon (or with an electric mixer) until creamy.

5. Add the egg and stir.

6. Add the vanilla and stir.

7. Choose a food-coloring color for this batch and add ½ teaspoon to identify this batch as Experiment A, then stir.

8. In a medium bowl, stir together the flour, baking powder, and salt.

9. Slowly add the flour mixture to the butter and sugar mixture and stir to form dough.

10. Repeat steps 4–9 for Experiment B. Be sure to use the **light brown sugar** in step 4 and a different color food coloring.

11. Repeat steps 4–9 for Experiment C. Be sure to use the **dark brown sugar** in step 4 and a different color food coloring.

12. Using a big spoon (or ice cream scoop), drop spoonfuls of dough from Experiment A in a row on the baking sheet. Leave 2 inches of space between each cookie.

13. Using a big spoon, drop spoonfuls of dough from Experiment B in a second row on the baking sheet. Leave 2 inches of space between each cookie.

14. Using a big spoon, drop spoonfuls of dough from Experiment C in a third row on the baking sheet. Leave 2 inches of space between each cookie.

15. Bake the cookies for 8 minutes, and then rotate the baking sheet in the oven. Bake for another 8 minutes (or until the edges are golden brown).

16. Once the cookies have finished baking, remove them from the oven.

17. Transfer to a rack to cool.

18. After the cookies have cooled, compare the taste and shape of each cookie.

WHAT DO YOU THINK?

> What was different about the appearance of the three types of cookies?
> How did the three different types of cookies taste? Which cookie was the sweetest?
> What will happen if we make a cookie with 50% white sugar and 50% brown sugar?
> Is there a limit to how much sugar we can add to the dough? What happens if we double or triple the amount of sugar?

HOW IT WORKS:

White sugar is made from a bunch of big molecules called sucrose, which you may recognize as one of the products from photosynthesis. During this process, green plants convert carbon dioxide into oxygen, in addition to producing sucrose (table sugar). We can extract this sugar out of sugarcane and sugar beet stems quite easily, before crystallizing the molecules into tiny sugar cubes.

When we pull the sucrose molecules out of the plants, a thick, dark syrup forms at the bottom of the container. This liquid is called molasses, which is an extremely viscous (thick and sticky), sugary liquid. Since viscous liquids pour incredibly slowly, bakers have developed a workaround: we can add molasses directly to our sugar.

It turns out that brown sugar is simply white sugar that has been coated in a thin layer of molasses. Light brown sugar is refined white sugar and 3.5% molasses, while dark brown sugar is really just white sugar with 6.5% molasses. Cookies made with brown sugar, especially dark brown sugar, are usually sweeter and have a richer taste, due to their higher concentrations of sugar molecules.

CHOCOLATE CHIP COOKIES

A NOTE FROM Kate: When I realized that I needed to make three different versions of a cookie for this experiment, I knew I had to pick my all-time favorite dessert: the chocolate chip cookie. I mean, is there anything better than a chocolate chip cookie fresh out of the oven? I hope you enjoy making—and tasting—this experiment!

Messiness Level: 2/3

Materials (for each experiment):

- ○ ½ cup unsalted butter, softened
- ○ Oven
- ○ Baking sheet
- ○ Parchment paper or nonstick cooking spray or silicone baking mats
- ○ ½ cup sugar
- ○ ½ cup brown sugar
- ○ Mixing bowl
- ○ Wooden spoon
- ○ 1 egg
- ○ ½ teaspoon vanilla
- ○ 1 cup flour
- ○ Baking soda/powder:
  EXPERIMENT A—THE CONTROL:
  [No baking soda/powder]
  EXPERIMENT B—BAKING SODA:
  ½ teaspoon baking soda
  EXPERIMENT C—BAKING POWDER:
  ½ teaspoon baking powder
- ○ ¼ teaspoon salt
- ○ ¾ cup chocolate chips
- ○ Big spoon
- ○ Cooling rack

PROTOCOL:

1. Remove the butter from the refrigerator and set aside to soften.

2. Heat the oven to 375°F.

3. Prepare a baking sheet (spray with nonstick cooking spray or line with parchment paper or silicone baking mat).

4. Mix the butter and sugar for Experiment A in a mixing bowl with a wooden spoon (or with an electric mixer) until creamy.

5. Add the egg and stir.

6. Add the vanilla and stir.

7. In a medium bowl, stir together the flour and salt. (Do not add any baking soda or baking powder.)

8. Slowly add the flour mixture to the butter and sugar mixture and stir to form dough.

9. Stir in the chocolate chips.

10. Label as Experiment A and set aside.

11. Repeat steps 4–9 for Experiment B. Be sure to add the **baking soda** in step 7.

12. Label the new dough as Experiment B and set aside.

13. Repeat steps 4–9 for Experiment C. Be sure to add the **baking powder** in step 7.

14. Label the new dough as Experiment C and set aside.

15. Using a big spoon (or ice cream scoop), drop spoonfuls of dough from Experiment A in a row on the baking sheet. Leave 2 inches of space between each cookie.
    PRO TIP: Use extra chocolate chips to label the first cookie in each row with a unique design. I labeled mine by adding 1, 2, or 3 chocolate chips to the top row of my baking sheet.

16. Using a big spoon, drop spoonfuls of dough from Experiment B in a second row on the baking sheet. Leave 2 inches of space between each cookie.

17. Using a big spoon, drop spoonfuls of dough from Experiment C in a third row on the baking sheet. Leave 2 inches of space between each cookie.

18. Bake the cookies for about 8 minutes. Rotate the baking sheet in the oven and bake for another 7–8 minutes (or until the cookies are golden brown).
    PRO TIP: If the cookies darken quickly around the edges, reduce the temperature to 350°F after 10 minutes.

19. Once the cookies have finished baking, remove them from the oven.

20. Transfer to a rack to cool.

21. Compare the final shapes and sizes of the cookies.

> Why did we perform one experiment without baking soda or baking powder?
> What was different about the shape, size, and color of the three batches of cookies?
> How did the taste of the three types of cookies differ?
> What will happen if we add ¼ teaspoon of baking soda and ¼ teaspoon of baking powder to the dough?
> What will happen to the shape of the cookies if we double the ingredients? Will they be taller or wider? Puffy or flat? Will their insides be as gooey?

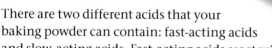

HOW IT WORKS:

Baking soda is a base (a molecule that has a pH greater than 7) that contains sodium bicarbonate. Like baking soda, baking powder has sodium bicarbonate, but it also contains a molecule called tartaric acid. An acid is the opposite of a base, which means tartaric acid has a pH less than 7.

There are two different acids that your baking powder can contain: fast-acting acids and slow-acting acids. Fast-acting acids react with the sodium bicarbonate in the mixing bowl and immediately begin to form carbon dioxide bubbles. Slow-acting acids need the heat from the oven to begin forming the carbon dioxide gas. Since baking powder contains both an acid and a base, it also has a little bit of cornstarch to make sure that the molecules don't react before you want them to.

Baking powder is a chemical leavening agent. This means that when baking powder is added to a dough, it increases the overall size of the delicious dessert. When you make a chocolate chip cookie, like in this experiment, the acid and the base in the baking powder react to form carbon dioxide gas. The gas helps to make the dough all light and fluffy, which is vital in a puffy chocolate chip cookie. Since baking soda does not contain an acid, it needs to react with an acid (like lemon or vinegar) in the cookie dough in order to affect the size of the cookie. But as you can see from the experiment, it has not only a dramatic effect on the overall color of the cookie, but also on the amount of time it takes to bake. The cookies in experiment B require less time in the oven than A and C, which is why they often appear darker and fluffier (at first).

ICE CREAM

A NOTE FROM KATE: In the fourth book of my fictional series *Kate the Chemist: The Birthday Blastoff,* Little Kate uses liquid nitrogen to make ice cream and save the day. Since most of us do not usually have liquid nitrogen in our homes, I wanted to come up with a similar experiment so that we could all partake in the fun!

MESSINESS LEVEL: 2/3

MATERIALS—EXPERIMENT A— ELECTRIC MIXER + FREEZER:

- ○ Metal mixing bowl
- ○ Freezer
- ○ 1¼ cups whole milk
- ○ ¾ cups sugar
- ○ Electric mixer
- ○ 2 cups heavy cream
- ○ 1 tablespoon vanilla
- ○ ¼ teaspoon salt
- ○ 9x13-inch baking pan

MATERIALS—EXPERIMENT B— PLASTIC BAG:

- ○ 4 cups crushed ice
- ○ ⅓ cup coarse salt
- ○ Gallon-size plastic baggie
- ○ 1 cup whole milk
- ○ 1 tablespoon sugar
- ○ ¾ teaspoon vanilla
- ○ 2 quart-size plastic baggies

EXPERIMENT A—ELECTRIC MIXER + FREEZER

PROtOCOL:

1. Put the metal mixing bowl into the freezer for 15 minutes.

2. Remove the mixing bowl from the freezer and quickly add milk and sugar.

3. Use an electric mixer to beat for 2 minutes.

4. Add heavy cream, vanilla, and salt.

5. Stir for another 30 seconds (or until a homogenous mixture forms).

6. Put the mixing bowl into the freezer for another 15 minutes.

7. Remove the mixing bowl from the freezer.

8. Pour the mixture into the 9x13-inch baking pan (or another deep, wide dish).

9. Put the baking pan into the freezer for 30 minutes.

10. Remove the baking pan from the freezer and pour the mixture into the mixing bowl.

11. Beat with an electric mixer for 3–4 minutes.

12. Return the mixture to the baking pan and place it back into the freezer for 30 minutes.

13. Repeat steps 10–12 until the milk mixture is completely frozen.

14. Analyze the appearance (texture, density, and color) of your ice cream.

15. Enjoy!

EXPERIMENT B—PLASTIC BAG

PROTOCOL:

1. Add milk, sugar, and vanilla to one quart-size plastic baggie.

2. Seal the quart-size bag and swoosh the ingredients around to combine the mixture.

3. Put the quart-size bag *into* the other, empty quart-size bag. Seal the second baggie and set aside.

4. Add ice and salt to the gallon-size plastic baggie.

5. Put the quart-size plastic baggies inside the gallon-size plastic baggie (the one with the ice and salt in it).

6. Squeeze all the air out of the gallon-size bag and seal it.

7. Check to make sure that all three bags are sealed well.

8. Put on heat-safe gloves or oven mitts.

9. Shake the ice cream mixture vigorously for 5–10 minutes (or until the ice cream has frozen). **Be careful. The mixture will become very cold.**

10. Analyze the appearance (texture, density, and color) of your ice cream.

11. Enjoy!

WHAT DO YOU THINK?

> Which experiment produced the best-tasting ice cream?
> Which ice cream was the easiest to make?
> How did the final ice cream differ for each experiment?
> Why did we need to salt the ice in order to make the ice cream in Experiment B?

HOW IT WORKS:

One of the best desserts on planet Earth is ice cream! It's sweet, creamy, and a perfect after-dinner treat. From a molecular perspective, ice cream is just a mixture of many different molecules, each of which is responsible for a different flavor that we experience. The triglycerides (fats) from the milk give the ice cream the creamy texture and flavors, the carbohydrates (sugars) make the ice cream taste sweet, and the sodium chloride (salt) gives it a hint of a salty taste.

But as you may have noticed, we didn't actually use any of the salt within the ice cream mixture in Experiment B. Instead, we added it to the plastic baggie that surrounded the milk mixture. This technique was imperative to Experiment B because we were able to take advantage of an important chemical phenomenon called freezing point depression. This situation occurs whenever a salt is added to water (or ice), and drops the overall freezing point of the mixture. Usually, water freezes at 0°C (32°F), but when we add salt to the water, we can drop the freezing point to about -20°C (-4°F). This may not seem like a big difference—however, we could see with our experiment how this small change in temperature is enough to freeze our ice cream without turning it into a solid ice block!

MINI-CHEESECAKES

A NOTE FROM KATE: I love cheesecakes so much that my mom threw me a cheesecake party to celebrate my graduation from high school. She made so many different types of cheesecakes, and we had such a great time. Every time I do this experiment, I'm reminded of the wonderful memories I have of that evening.

MESSINESS LEVEL: 2/3

MATERIALS:

- ○ Oven
- ○ Muffin pan
- ○ Butter for greasing (or nonstick cooking spray or cupcake liners) + 3 tablespoons butter, melted
- ○ 1 cup graham cracker crumbs
- ○ Small bowl
- ○ 2 tablespoons + ½ cup sugar
- ○ Spoon
- ○ Cooling rack

MATERIALS—EXPERIMENT A— ALL CREAM CHEESE:

- ○ 8 ounces cream cheese (with fat)
- ○ ¼ cup sugar
- ○ Mixing bowl
- ○ 1 egg
- ○ ½ teaspoon vanilla
- ○ Spoon

MATERIALS—EXPERIMENT B— CREAM CHEESE + SOUR CREAM:

- ○ 4 ounces cream cheese (with fat)
- ○ ½ cup sour cream
- ○ ¼ cup sugar
- ○ Mixing bowl
- ○ 1 egg
- ○ ½ teaspoon vanilla
- ○ Spoon

PROTOCOL:

1. Take the cream cheese and sour cream out of the refrigerator. Set aside.

2. Heat the oven to 350°F.

3. Grease muffin pan with butter (or nonstick cooking spray, or use cupcake liners).

4. Add melted butter and the crushed graham crackers to the small bowl.

5. Add 2 tablespoons of sugar to the mixture.

6. Stir the mixture together until the graham crackers are evenly coated.

7. Add 1 spoonful of the graham cracker mixture to each muffin cup. Be as consistent as possible.

8. Use the back of the spoon (or the bottom of a small cup) to push the crust into the muffin cups. The crust should feel firm.

9. Check to make sure the bottoms of the crust are relatively flat.

10. Bake for 5 minutes.

11. Remove from the oven and set aside on the cooling rack.

EXPERIMENT A—ALL CREAM CHEESE

PROTOCOL:

1. Cream together the cream cheese and sugar in the mixing bowl by hand (or with an electric mixer).

2. Add the egg and stir.

3. Add the vanilla and stir.

4. Pour the mixture evenly into half the muffin cups (over the baked graham cracker crusts).

5. Use a knife to carve an A into one of the cheesecakes (or use a few chocolate chips or blueberries).

6. Analyze the appearance, texture, and density of the cheesecakes.

EXPERIMENT B—CREAM CHEESE + SOUR CREAM

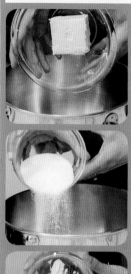

PROTOCOL:

1. Cream together the cream cheese, sugar, and sour cream in the mixing bowl by hand (or with an electric mixer).

2. Add the egg and stir.

3. Add the vanilla and stir.

4. Pour the mixture evenly into the remaining empty muffin cups (over the baked graham cracker crusts).

5. Use a knife to carve a B into one of the cheesecakes (or use a few chocolate chips or blueberries).

6. Analyze the appearance, texture, and density of the cheesecakes.

PROTOCOL (CONTINUED):

12. Bake the Mini-Cheesecakes for 15–20 minutes (or until the centers just stop jiggling).

13. Remove from the oven, and analyze the appearance, texture, and density of the cheesecakes.

14. Cool on a rack for about 30 minutes.

15. Put the Mini-Cheesecakes in the refrigerator for 2–3 hours (or until completely chilled).

16. Analyze the appearance, texture, density, and **taste** of the cheesecakes!

> Why did we prebake the pie crusts?
> What would happen if we used fat-free cream cheese?
> How did the appearance of the two cheesecakes differ before they were baked? What about after they were baked?
> Which cheesecake solidified fastest in the oven? Would it have been better to use two different muffin pans?
> Which cheesecake had the fluffiest texture? Was it the same one that had the best taste?

HOW IT WORKS:

Cream cheese is a delicious dairy product that is produced from the combination of milk and acid. With a little hard work, you can actually make your own cream cheese just by combining 4 cups of whole milk and 2 tablespoons lemon juice or vinegar. Just like with buttermilk, the acid from the lemon (citric acid) or the vinegar (acetic acid) triggers a chemical reaction that curdles the milk. Manufacturers often use lactic acid to get the perfect sour taste of their cream cheese (and a lot more cream). After the milk has curdled, the mixture is processed heavily to obtain the perfectly smooth texture of cream cheese.

In this experiment, we also investigated how sour cream can be used to make a cheesecake filling. Just like cream cheese, sour cream is frequently made by adding lactic acid to the dairy product. The major difference is that cream cheese uses milk as a starting product, whereas sour cream uses cream. The lactic acid bacteria is added to the cream, causing it to ferment and become incredibly sour. This process naturally thickens the cream to give it the yogurt-like texture.

Sour cream and cream cheese both work for cheesecakes because they are very similar dairy products. Cream cheese is traditionally used over sour cream due to its extremely high fat content. The triglyceride molecules in the fat give the cheesecakes the creamy texture and delicious taste. However, some people actually prefer the sour taste associated with the sour cream cheesecakes over the rich flavor of pure cream cheese cheesecakes. What do you think? Which one did you prefer?

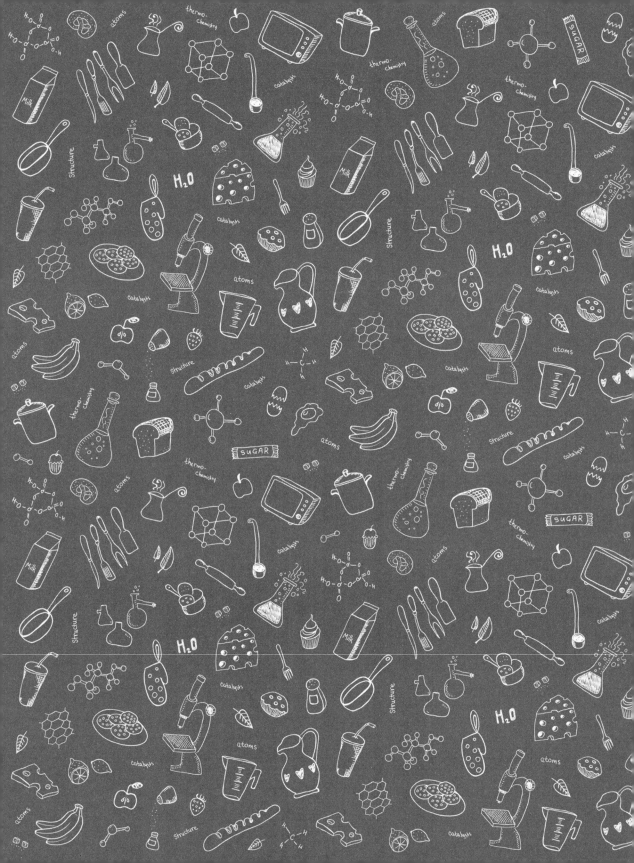